Step-by-Step Classic Kitchen

A hundred graded recipes with kitchen hints and wine guide

**SELECT
EDITIONS**

Step-by-Step Classic Kitchen

Vegetables

From the first tender carrots or young broad beans of spring, the sun-ripened tomatoes and courgettes of autumn, to firm winter favourites like Brussels sprouts or celery – the opportunities for rich and varied vegetable-based dishes throughout the year are endless. And as more and more exotic varieties are finding their way to our shops and supermarkets – aubergines, artichokes, salsify, pumpkins – there are always new tastes to discover and new ways of cooking vegetables to learn.

Vegetables, both raw and cooked, form an essential part of our diet, providing us with many necessary nutrients, and are our chief source of vitamins. Their rich variety of colour and flavour will enhance the attractiveness of any meal. Yet all too often we ignore this vital area of the art of cooking and are content to serve dull, badly cooked vegetables, usually reduced by too much boiling to a tasteless watery mush, to the detriment of all the other courses.

This book will change all that. It is designed to restore vegetables to their rightful and essential place in the planning of a meal. Indeed, many of the dishes described here can be served as meals in their own right – a whole cabbage stuffed with a delicious savoury filling, a tasty ratatouille, leeks prepared with cheese and ham, delicately-flavoured soufflés, or a hearty, warming stew of beans and bacon. To help even the most inexperienced devise a well-balanced and appetizing menu, advice is given on complementing meat and vegetable dishes – lentil purée with pork, for example, or celeriac with game – and there are plenty of tips on attractive and unusual garnishes.

Used as we are in this country to a dreary regime of boiled vegetables, you may be surprised by how many different ways there are of preparing them: in purées or soufflés, blanched or braised, sautéed or baked in the oven and served with innumerable different sauces. There are clear, helpful instructions to guide you through all these methods, and the easy-to-follow, step-by-step recipes will ensure that your cooking of these new and exciting dishes will turn out a success every time.

Table of Contents

> Each dish is followed by its total preparation and cooking time. (See note 1 on facing page.)
>
> The star (★) system used throughout the book, indicating the degree of simplicity or difficulty of each recipe, is as follows:
>
> ★ Very easy   ★★ Easy   ★★★ Difficult

Artichokes

		page
Gratin of Stuffed Artichokes (1 hr)	★★	6
Soufflé of Artichoke Hearts (1 hr 40 min)	★★★	6
Artichokes with Mint (1 hr)	★★	8
Artichokes Roman-Style with Herbs (1 hr 15 min)	★★	8
Artichokes Palermo-Style (55 min)	★	8
Artichokes Stuffed with Rice (1 hr 20 min)	★★★	9
Artichoke and Potato Stew (50 min)	★★	9
Artichokes Peasant-Style (1 hr)	★★	10
Artichoke Fritters (40 min)	★★	10
Artichokes with Prawns (30 min)	★	10

Asparagus

Asparagus in a Cheese Omelette (1 hr)	★★	12
Asparagus and Mushroom Salad (40 min)	★	12
Asparagus with Hollandaise Sauce (1 hr)	★★★	13
Asparagus Gratin Hungarian-Style (50 min)	★★	13
Asparagus Gratin with Ham (50 min)	★★	14
Asparagus with Egg, Lemon and Herbs (35 min)	★	14

Aubergines (Egg Plant)

Sautéed Aubergines (1 hr 15 min)	★	16
Ratatouille (Aubergine, Pepper and Courgette Stew) (1 hr 30 min)	★★	16
Ratatouille Sicilian-Style (1 hr 10 min)	★★	17
Ratatouille with Celery and Olives (40 min)	★	17
Stuffed Aubergines with Cheese (1 hr 5 min)	★★	18
Vegetable Cake with Marjoram (1 hr 25 min)	★★	18
Aubergines with Parmesan Cheese (1 hr 50 min)	★★	20
Aubergine Fritters (2 hr 50 min)	★★★	20

Seakale (Chard)

Seakale Gratin (1 hr 5 min)	★★	21

Cardoons (Globe Artichokes)

Gratin of Cardoons (1 hr 50 min)	★★	28
Cardoons with Egg Sauce (1 hr 45 min)	★★	29
Cardoons with Beef Marrow (1 hr 50 min)	★★	29

Carrots

Carrots with Gruyère Cheese (50 min)	★	24
Purée of Carrots and Potatoes (1 hr)	★★	24
Sweet and Sour Carrots (40 min)	★	24
Carrots with Sultanas (1 hr 10 min)	★	25
Purée of Carrots with Milk (1 hr)	★	25
Peasant-Style Soup (55 min)	★★	25

Celery and Celeriac

Celeriac with Lemon (40 min)	★★	21
Braised Celery Hearts with Olives (50 min)	★★	22
Purée of Celeriac (50 min)	★★	22

Cèpes (Mushrooms)

Cèpes with Mint (55 min)	★★	30
Cèpes with Shallots (35 min)	★	30

Cabbage

Stuffed Cabbage (2 hr 30 min)	★★★	32
Stuffed Cabbage Leaves (1 hr 20 min)	★★★	32
Cabbage in Vinegar (55 min)	★	33
Braised Cabbage with Tomato (50 min)	★	33
Cabbage with Herbs, Italian-Style (1 hr 20 min)	★★	36
Flemish Red Cabbage (1 hr)	★★	36
Sweet and Sour Cabbage (1 hr 30 min)	★★	38
Cabbage with Cheese Sauce (50 min)	★★	40

Brussels Sprouts

Brussels Sprouts with Cream (35 min)	★★	33
Brussels Sprouts with Ham (45 min)	★	40

Cauliflower

Cold Cauliflower with Scampi (1 hr)	★★	34
Cauliflower with Two Kinds of Paprika (40 min)	★★	34
Purée of Cauliflower (40 min)	★	36
Cauliflower Fritters (45 min)	★★★	37
Cauliflower with Almonds (30 min)	★★	37
Cauliflower Cheese (35 min)	★★	38
Sautéed Cauliflower with Onions and Sausagemeat (30 min)	★	38

Courgettes

Gratin of Courgettes (50 min)	★★	26
Courgettes Stuffed with Tuna (1 hr 5 min)	★★	26
Courgettes with Veal (45 min)	★★	28

Chicory

Chicory Sautéed with Cream (50 min)	★★	44
Chicory with Milk (35 min)	★★	44
Chicory and Walnut Salad (15 min)	★	44

Spinach

Baked Spinach with Eggs and Cream (50 min)	★★	40
Spinach Cake (1 hr 15 min)	★★★	41
Green Cake (50 min)	★★	41
Spinach with Tomatoes (40 min)	★★	42
Spinach Gratin (40 min)	★★	42

Fennel

Fennel with Mayonnaise (35 min)	★★	46
Fennel with Black Olives (30 min)	★	46
Fennel Salad with Roquefort Cheese (15 min)	★	46

Broad Beans

page

Broad Beans Peasant-Style *(1 hr 20 min)* ★★ 45
Broad Beans Roman-Style *(1 hr 5 min)* ★★ 45
Broad Beans with Peppers *(1 hr 5 min)* ★ 45

Haricot Beans

White Bean Stew *(1 hr 25 min)* ★★ 48
Haricot Beans with Vegetables ★★ 49
(1 hr 45 min)
White Bean Salad, served warm ★ 49
(1 hr 15 min)
Fresh Haricot Beans with Bacon ★★ 50
(1 hr 50 min)

French Beans

French Beans with Parsley *(45 min)* ★ 48
Purée of French Beans *(1 hr 50 min)* ★★ 48
French Beans with Yogurt *(40 min)* ★★ 50
French Beans with Four Kinds of Cheese ★★ 52
(50 min)
French Beans with Anchovies *(40 min)* ★ 52
Butter Beans with Tomato and Bacon ★ 52
(40 min)

Lentils

Lentils Peasant-Style *(2 hr 10 min)* ★★ 53
Lentils with Bacon *(1 hr 40 min)* ★ 53

Turnips

Purée of Turnip *(50 min)* ★ 54
Glazed Turnips *(55 min)* ★ 54
Stuffed Turnips *(2 hr)* ★★★ 54

Onions

Egg and Onion Pie *(1 hr 15 min)* ★★★ 56
Onion and Asparagus Soufflé *(1 hr)* ★★★ 56
Glazed White Onions *(1 hr 20 min)* ★ 57
Flaky Onion Tart *(1 hr)* ★★ 57
Pickled Onions *(1 hr 15 min)* ★ 57
Onions Stuffed with Salmon ★★★ 58
(1 hr 20 min)
Onions Stuffed with Tuna *(1 hr)* ★★★ 58

Peas

Fresh Green Peas with Bacon *(45 min)* ★ 66
Purée of Peas *(20 min)* ★★ 66
Casserole of Spring Vegetables ★★ 66
(1 hr 5 min)

Leeks

Gratin of Leeks with Ham *(1 hr)* ★★ 72
Leeks with Tomato and Cheese *(45 min)* ★★ 72

page

Leeks with Red or White Wine ★ 73
(1 hr 55 min)

Peppers

Peppers Stuffed with Mozzarella ★★★ 69
(1 hr 15 min)
Grilled Peppers *(50 min)* ★ 69
Stuffed Peppers with Cheese Sauce *(1 hr)* ★★ 70
Braised Peppers with Capers *(50 min)* ★ 70
Peppers Stuffed with Ham *(1 hr)* ★★ 70

Chickpeas

Chickpeas Peasant-Style *(2 hr 30 min)* ★ 68
Chickpeas Milanese *(2 hr 45 min)* ★★ 68
Chickpeas with Pork Ribs *(2 hr 10 min)* ★★ 68

Potatoes

Potatoes with Milk and Cream ★ 60
(1 hr 10 min)
Potato Purée with Two Kinds of Cheese ★★ 60
(1 hr 10 min)
Potato Surprise with Mushrooms and ★★★ 61
Tomato Sauce *(1 hr)*
Potato Vermicelli *(35 min)* ★ 61
Potatoes Stuffed with Tuna *(45 min)* ★★ 62
Potato Gâteau *(1 hr 5 min)* ★★★ 62
Potatoes Dauphinois, Baked with ★★ 64
Cheese *(1 hr 45 min)*
Potato and Cheese Croquettes *(1 hr)* ★★★ 64
Lacy Potato Cakes (Dentelles) *(35 min)* ★★ 65
Jansson's Potatoes with Anchovies ★★ 65
and Cream *(1 hr 30 min)*

Pumpkins

Stuffed Pumpkin *(1 hr 30 min)* ★★★ 73
Pumpkin Soufflé *(1 hr 10 min)* ★★★ 74
Baked Pumpkin *(1 hr 10 min)* ★★ 74

Green Salads

Braised Lettuces with Beef Marrow ★★ 76
(35 min)
Braised Endives with Leeks *(35 min)* ★ 76
Stuffed Lettuce Leaves *(1 hr 20 min)* ★★★ 77

Salsify

Salsify Sautéed in Butter *(1 hr 15 min)* ★ 77

Tomatoes

Tomatoes Stuffed with Rice *(50 min)* ★★ 78
Tomatoes with Garlic and Parsley ★ 78
(1 hr 20 min)

Notes: Getting the Best out of this Book

1. The preparation times given in the Table of Contents and with each recipe are minimum times: they will vary according to the cook's ability and the equipment available.

2. It is best to use double cream for most recipes – it is the nearest equivalent to French cream. Remember also that the French use unsalted butter, and this is assumed in the recipes unless otherwise stated.

3. It is always best to use red or white wine vinegar in the recipes where vinegar is required; the results will not be the same if you use malt vinegar. In the same way, freshly ground black pepper should always be used in preference to ready-ground pepper.

4. Oven temperatures. The following are Gas, Fahrenheit and Centigrade equivalents:

Gas	¼	½	1	2	3	4	5	6	7	8	9
°F	225	250	275	300	325	350	375	400	425	450	475
°C	110	120	140	160	170	180	190	200	220	230	250

5. It is important when using these recipes to follow the exact proportions. A set of kitchen scales, measuring jug, glass and spoons are essential. Follow either metric *or* avoirdupois measurements in each recipe.

6. To help you choose the right wine for your meal, see page 80.

Artichauts Farcis Gratinés
Gratin of Stuffed Artichokes

Serves 4. Preparation: 20 min Cooking: 40 min

★ ★

- ○ **8 young artichokes**
- ○ **50g (2 oz) smoked bacon**
- ○ **100g (4 oz) small sausages or sausagemeat**
- ○ **1 egg**
- ○ **1 peeled garlic clove**
- ○ **10 sprigs parsley**
- ○ **30ml (2 tbls) breadcrumbs**
- ○ **50g (2 oz) grated Parmesan or Gruyère cheese**
- ○ **juice of 1 lemon**
- ○ **60ml (4 tbls) oil**
- ○ **200ml (7 fl oz) water**
- ○ **salt and pepper**

1. Wash the artichokes and remove the toughest leaves. Slice off the remaining leaves halfway from the top. Spread the centre leaves and remove the choke to make room for the stuffing. Cut the stalk off near the base. Soak the artichokes in water containing lemon juice.
2. Prepare stuffing. Skin the sausages and mash them with a fork. Dice the bacon. Chop the garlic and parsley finely. Put all the ingredients in a bowl, add the egg and breadcrumbs, season with salt and pepper and mix well.
3. Set the oven at 200°C (385°F; gas mark 5½).
4. Pour the oil and water into a gratin dish, arrange the artichokes in it and place in oven for 40 minutes.
5. Serve very hot, or allow to cool.

If served cold, accompany with thin slices of red pepper and small spring onions.

Soufflé de Fonds d'Artichauts
Soufflé of Artichoke Hearts

Serves 4. Preparation and cooking: 1 hr 40 min

★ ★ ★

- ○ **6 artichokes 200g (7 oz) each**
- ○ **4 eggs (separated)**
- ○ **250ml (9 fl oz) milk**
- ○ **15ml (1 tbls) flour**
- ○ **30ml (2 tbls) grated Gruyère cheese**
- ○ **70g (3 oz) butter**
- ○ **juice of 1 lemon**
- ○ **salt**
- ○ **pinch nutmeg**

1. Wash and trim the artichokes. Bring some water with lemon juice added to the boil, add salt and cook the artichokes in it for 40 minutes, until they are very tender. Then put under cold running water and remove the leaves and choke.
2. Prepare béchamel sauce. Melt 50g (2 oz) butter in a saucepan; add flour, turning in with a wooden spoon, then add milk, stirring continuously. Add salt and nutmeg. Cook for 10 minutes stirring all the time. Remove from heat and allow to cool.
3. Meanwhile, put the artichoke hearts through a fine sieve or, better still, in the blender to get rid of all the fibres. Incorporate the purée with the béchamel sauce, mixing well. Add egg yolks and grated cheese.
4. Set the oven at 190°C (365°F; gas mark 4½).
5. Beat egg whites until stiff and fold in to the mixture gently.
6. Butter a soufflé dish of a capacity 1½ times the volume of the mixture. Pour in the mixture and put in oven for 35 minutes. Serve immediately.

Steaming vegetables – or cooking à l'anglaise *– is a very common practice in England. In France, only potatoes are normally cooked like this and are called* pommes de terre à l'anglaise. *This method is highly recommended, easy and quick, and requires no great skill. All you need is a special hermetically sealed pan to prevent any loss of heat. The water must boil continuously to ensure sufficient steam pressure. Steamed vegetables are delicious eaten hot with a knob of butter, or cold with a salad. This method of cooking is also best for soufflés, purées or gratins as the vegetables are not full of water.*

Artichauts à la Menthe

Serves 4. Preparation: 20 min Cooking: 40 min

Artichokes with Mint

★★

- ○ **8 young artichokes**
- ○ **½ lemon**
- ○ **100g (4 oz) breadcrumbs**
- ○ **15ml (1 tbls) chopped parsley**
- ○ **2 anchovy fillets, canned**
- ○ **8 mint leaves**
- ○ **90ml (6 tbls) olive oil**
- ○ **200ml (7 fl oz) water**
- ○ **salt and pepper**

1. Wash the artichokes and drain them. Cut 1cm (½ inch) off the tops of the leaves. Cut off the stalks near the base and remove the toughest leaves. Rub the artichokes with lemon.
2. Prepare stuffing. Mix the breadcrumbs, parsley and half the oil in a bowl. Mash the anchovies and add to stuffing. Add salt and pepper.
3. Set the oven at 195°C (375°F; gas mark 5).
4. Spread the leaves slightly and place some of the stuffing in each artichoke.
5. Put the remaining oil with the water and the mint leaves in a gratin dish. Arrange artichokes on top and season with salt.
6. Cook in oven for 40 minutes and serve hot from the dish.

Artichauts à la Romaine

Serves 4. Preparation: 15 min Cooking: 1 hr

Artichokes Roman-Style with Herbs

★★

- ○ **8 very tender artichokes**
- ○ **juice of 1 lemon**
- ○ **3 peeled garlic cloves**
- ○ **4 mint leaves**
- ○ **10 sprigs parsley**
- ○ **50g (2 oz) breadcrumbs**
- ○ **150ml (5 fl oz) olive oil**
- ○ **salt and pepper**

1. Cut off the artichoke stalks 3cm (1¼ inches) from the base and remove the tough outer leaves. Slice through, at one go, the remaining leaves one-third from the top. Wash artichokes and leave to soak in water to which the lemon juice has been added.
2. Meanwhile, prepare a mixture of finely chopped garlic, mint and parsley. Add breadcrumbs and 30ml (2 tbls) olive oil. Add salt and pepper.
3. Drain artichokes and slightly spread the leaves. Put a little stuffing in each heart.
4. Set the oven at 180°C (350°F; gas mark 4).
5. Arrange artichokes, heads down, in an ovenproof dish. Sprinkle with remaining oil and half-cover with water. Add salt and pepper. Put into oven for 1 hour, basting frequently.
6. Serve the artichokes hot, cold or luke warm. They are delicious in every way.

Artichauts comme à Palerme

Serves 4. Preparation: 15 min Cooking: 40 min

Artichokes Palermo-Style

 ★

- ○ **8 young artichokes (with a purplish colour)**
- ○ **2 garlic cloves**
- ○ **10 sprigs parsley**
- ○ **50g (2 oz) Parmesan cheese**
- ○ **30ml (2 tbls) breadcrumbs**
- ○ **juice of 1 lemon**
- ○ **100ml (3½ fl oz) oil**
- ○ **100ml (3½ fl oz) water**
- ○ **20g (¾ oz) butter**
- ○ **salt and pepper**

1. Wash the artichokes, removing the toughest leaves. Slice through the remaining leaves in one go, one-third from the top. Cut into 8 and remove choke. Leave to soak in water with lemon juice added. Peel the garlic and chop finely. Chop the parsley roughly. Drain artichokes.
2. Heat the oil in a heavy pan. Add the butter and artichokes. Brown slightly, then add the garlic and parsley mixture. Add salt and pepper. Pour in water and cook for 35 minutes over a low heat.
3. At the end of this time, mix the Parmesan cheese and breadcrumbs and sprinkle over artichokes. Cook for a further 5 minutes and serve.

Artichauts Farcis au Riz

Serves 4. Preparation: 35 min Cooking: 45 min

Artichokes Stuffed with Rice

★ ★ ★

- ○ **8 artichokes**
- ○ **4 thin rashers of smoked bacon**
- ○ **60ml (4 tbls) cooked rice**
- ○ **100g (4 oz) raw ham**
- ○ **150g (6 oz) button mushrooms**
- ○ **100g (4 oz) sausagemeat**
- ○ **15ml (1 tbls) chopped parsley**
- ○ **4 ripe tomatoes**
- ○ **50g (2 oz) grated Gruyère cheese**
- ○ **1 small onion**
- ○ **50g (2 oz) butter**
- ○ **juice of 1 lemon**
- ○ **100ml (3½ fl oz) dry white wine**
- ○ **salt and pepper**

1. Wash artichokes and remove toughest leaves. Slice through the remaining leaves in one go, one-third from top. Spread the centre leaves to stuff, and remove choke. Cut off stalk near base. Bring water to boil in saucepan, add salt and lemon juice. Blanch artichokes for 5 minutes, then drain.
2. Peel onion and chop small. Chop ham. Trim the mushrooms and slice finely. Prepare the tomatoes by plunging in boiling water for 30 seconds, then hold under cold running water and peel. Cut in two, press to remove seeds, chop into large pieces, then mash roughly with a fork.
3. Melt 30g (1¼ oz) butter in a large frying pan. Lightly brown onion then add the ham, mushrooms and sausagemeat which has been mashed with a fork. Brown everything lightly. Add tomatoes to frying pan, then the salt and pepper. Cook over strong heat, turning often, until the liquid has completely evaporated. Remove from heat, add the rice, cheese and parsley, and mix well.
4. Set the oven at 205°C (400°F; gas mark 6). Stuff the artichokes. Cut each rasher of bacon in two to cover artichokes. Grease a gratin dish with remaining butter and arrange artichokes on it. Moisten with wine and cook in oven for 40 minutes, adding some spoonfuls of water to the dish if necessary. Remove from oven and serve.

Artichauts et Pommes de Terre en Cocotte

Serves 4. Preparation: 20 min Cooking: 30 min approx

Artichoke and Potato Stew

★ ★

- ○ **4 young artichokes**
- ○ **8 small potatoes**
- ○ **2 peeled garlic cloves**
- ○ **10 sprigs parsley**
- ○ **1 stock cube**
- ○ **½ litre (18 fl oz; 1 pint) hot water**
- ○ **juice of 1 lemon**
- ○ **60ml (4 tbls) oil**
- ○ **salt and pepper**

1. Wash the artichokes and remove toughest leaves. Slice through remaining leaves in one go, one-third from top. Cut into 8, remove choke, leave to soak in water with lemon juice added.
2. Peel and wash potatoes. Cut into 4 and soak in cold water.
3. Finely chop parsley and garlic. Dissolve stock cube in hot water. Drain artichokes and potatoes.
4. Place the oil in a heavy pan, add garlic and parsley mixture, potatoes and artichokes. Season with salt and pepper and cover with stock. Bring to the boil and cover.
5. Cook for 20 to 25 minutes until all the stock has disappeared and artichokes are tender. If any stock is left after cooking, reduce it over a high heat. Serve very hot.

Artichauts à la Paysanne

Serves 4. Preparation: 20 min Cooking: 40 min

Artichokes Peasant-Style

★★

- ○ **8 artichokes**
- ○ **300g (11 oz) small onions**
- ○ **100g (4 oz) pitted green olives**
- ○ **250g (9 oz) ripe tomatoes**
- ○ **2 peeled garlic cloves**
- ○ **15ml (1 tbls) capers**
- ○ **juice of 1 lemon**
- ○ **45ml (3 tbls) oil**
- ○ **salt and pepper**

1. Wash tomatoes, cut into 4, put through sieve or blender. Put on one side. Wash and drain artichokes. Remove tough outer leaves and slice through remaining leaves halfway down. Remove choke. Soak artichokes in water with lemon juice added. Cut into 8. Peel onions. Chop together very finely garlic and one small onion.
2. Heat the oil in a heavy pan. Add to it the garlic and onion mixture, the artichokes, and the whole onions. Season with salt and pepper. Cook for 10 minutes over a low heat, turning often.
3. Pour the tomato purée into the pan. Cover and cook for a further 10 minutes before adding capers and olives. Allow to simmer for 20 minutes. Serve hot or cold.

Artichauts en Beignets

Serves 4. Preparation and cooking: 40 min approx

Artichoke Fritters

★★

- ○ **8 small artichokes**
- ○ **2 eggs**
- ○ **200ml (7 fl oz) milk**
- ○ **80g (3¼ oz) flour**
- ○ **½ lemon**
- ○ **salt**
- ○ **oil for frying**

1. Wash artichokes and remove outer leaves. Slice through remaining leaves halfway down; leave 1cm (½ inch) stalk. Cut artichokes into 4, removing choke, and sprinkle with lemon juice. Blanch for 10 minutes in salted boiling water.
2. Meanwhile, prepare mixture for frying. In a bowl, mix the flour and milk, using a whisk to avoid lumps. Add eggs and salt. Mix again. When artichokes are blanched, strain them and add to the mixture.
3. Heat oil in a large frying pan. When smoke appears, drop in the artichoke fritters and cook until brown, about 3 minutes each. To ensure perfect cooking, do not put too many fritters into pan at the same time.
4. When fritters are well browned, place on absorbent paper and keep warm until ready to serve.

Artichauts aux Crevettes

Serves 4. Preparation and cooking: 30 min

Artichokes with Prawns

★

- ○ **4 artichokes**
- ○ **200g (7 oz) peeled prawns**
- ○ **100ml (3½ fl oz) fresh cream**
- ○ **10ml (2 tsp) mustard**
- ○ **15ml (1 tbls) oil**
- ○ **10 sprigs parsley**
- ○ **6 stalks chives**
- ○ **1 sprig tarragon**
- ○ **1 lemon**
- ○ **salt and pepper**

1. Wash artichokes and remove the tough outer leaves. Slice through remaining leaves one-third from top. Spread centre leaves slightly and remove choke. Cut off stalk near the base. Rub with half a lemon. Cook for 20 minutes in salted boiling water.
2. Chop herbs. Cut prawns into rounds.
3. Put mustard, salt, pepper and juice of ½ lemon into a dish. Mix in oil and cream, beating with fork. Add the prawns and herbs.
4. When artichokes are ready, drain. Allow to cool and stuff with mixture. Serve cold.

Asperges Lolita
Asparagus in a Cheese Omelette

Serves 4. Preparation and cooking: 1 hr

★ ★

○ **1kg (2¼ lb) thin green asparagus**
○ **2 eggs**
○ **100ml (3½ fl oz) milk**
○ **100ml (3½ fl oz) fresh double cream**
○ **100g (4 oz) Emmenthal cheese**
○ **20ml (4 tsp) oil**
○ **50g (2 oz) butter**
○ **salt and pepper**
○ **pinch nutmeg**
○ **15ml (1 tbls) coarse salt**

1. Place a large saucepan, three-quarters full of water, over high heat, add coarse salt, and bring to the boil.
2. Scrape or peel and wash the asparagus. Cut into even lengths and tie together. Place the bundle in the boiling water, which should come 1cm (½ inch) below the asparagus tips so that they are not spoiled during cooking. Simmer gently for about 20 minutes. Check cooking by pricking with a knife which should go in easily.
4. Meanwhile, prepare an omelette: beat the eggs with the cream and milk in a bowl. Add salt, pepper, and nutmeg. Divide the mixture to make 4 small omelettes.
5. Add 5ml (1 tsp) of oil to a small frying pan. When the oil is hot, pour one-quarter of the mixture into the pan and cook gently for 3 minutes. Turn the omelette immediately, like a thick pancake. Slide it onto a plate then replace it in the pan to cook on the other side for another 2 minutes. Cook the other 3 omelettes in the same way.
6. When the asparagus is cooked, remove from water, untie and drain on a rack. Divide into 4.
7. Slice the Emmenthal cheese thinly.
8. Set the oven at 220°C (425°F; gas mark 7) and butter a gratin dish.
9. Garnish each omelette with slices of Emmenthal cheese and roll around each portion of asparagus. Place these parcels in a gratin dish and put in the oven for 5 minutes so that the cheese melts. Serve immediately.

Serve ketchups and sauces separately. Garnish with slices of tomato.

Salade d'Asperges et de Champignons
Asparagus and Mushroom Salad

Serves 4. Preparation: 20 min
Cooking: 20 min

★

○ **500g (1 lb 2 oz) blanched asparagus**
○ **250g (9 oz) fresh button mushrooms**
○ **juice of 1 lemon**
○ **2 tomatoes**
○ **30ml (2 tbls) vinegar**
○ **60ml (4 tbls) oil**
○ **5ml (1 tsp) mild paprika**
○ **salt and pepper**
○ **5ml (1 tsp) coarse salt**

1. Place large saucepan three-quarters full of water over a high heat, and add coarse salt.
2. Scrape or peel and wash asparagus. Cut into pieces 3cm (1 inch) long – only use top two-thirds of each spear.
3. When the water boils plunge in the asparagus and simmer gently for about 20 minutes.
4. Meanwhile wash, dry and thinly slice the tomatoes. Trim the mushrooms and wipe with a cloth. Slice finely and sprinkle with lemon juice.
5. Strain asparagus in a colander.
6. Prepare vinaigrette with oil and vinegar. Add paprika, salt and pepper.
7. Mix tomatoes and asparagus in the salad bowl. Drain mushrooms and add them. Sprinkle with vinaigrette and put into refrigerator for 30 minutes.

Asperges Sauce Hollandaise

Serves 4. Preparation and cooking: 1 hr

Asparagus with Hollandaise Sauce

★★★

○ **1kg (2¼ lb) asparagus**
○ **100ml (3½ fl oz) wine vinegar**
○ **5ml (1 tsp) milled pepper**
○ **3 egg yolks**
○ **200g (7 oz) butter**
○ **juice of 1 lemon**
○ **200ml (7 fl oz) water**
○ **salt**
○ **15ml (1 tbls) coarse salt**

1. Place large saucepan three-quarters full of water on a high heat, and add coarse salt.
2. Scrape or peel and wash asparagus. Cut into equal lengths and tie in a bundle.
3. When water boils, place bundle upright in saucepan. The water should come to 1cm (½ inch) below the asparagus tips so that they are not spoiled during cooking. Simmer gently for about 20 minutes. Check cooking by pricking with a knife which should go in easily.
4. Meanwhile prepare Hollandaise sauce: put vinegar and pepper into a saucepan, bring to the boil and evaporate liquid until only 5ml (1 tsp) remains. Remove from heat and leave to cool. Away from heat add the egg yolks one by one, beating with a whisk, then add the water. Put saucepan back on a gentle heat and heat slowly, beating continuously. Remove again from heat, allowing the sauce formed to cool.
5. When asparagus is ready, remove from water, undo binding and drain on rack.
6. Prepare clarified butter: melt butter over low heat and skim. Use the transparent layer of butter and throw away the deposit which forms at the bottom. Allow to cool.
7. When the butter is at the same temperature as the sauce, blend together gently, beating lightly. Then pass the sauce through a very fine sieve, and add salt and lemon juice.
8. Arrange the asparagus on a suitable dish with a rack. Serve Hollandaise sauce separately – it should be lukewarm and of a firm consistency like mayonnaise.

Asperges Gratinées à la Hongroise

Serves 4.
Preparation and cooking: 50 min

Asparagus Gratin Hungarian-Style

★★

○ **1kg (2¼ lb) asparagus**
○ **2 egg yolks**
○ **15ml (1 tbls) sugar**
○ **30ml (2 tbls) flour**
○ **250g (9 oz) fresh cream**
○ **30ml (2 tbls) breadcrumbs**
○ **15ml (1 tbls) coarse salt**
○ **salt**

1. Place a large saucepan three-quarters full of water over a high heat, and add coarse salt.
2. Scrape or peel, wash and tie asparagus in a bundle.
3. When the water boils, place the bundle upright in saucepan. The water should come 1cm (½ inch) below the tips so that they are not spoilt during cooking. Simmer gently for 20 minutes. Check cooking by pricking with a knife which should go in easily.
4. Meanwhile, prepare sauce: in a bowl mix the egg yolks, salt, sugar and flour with whisk. Add fresh cream and beat further to mix well.
5. Set oven at 195°C (375°F; gas mark 5).
6. When the asparagus is cooked, remove from the water, tie and drain on rack.
7. Butter an ovenproof dish, arrange asparagus in it, and cover with sauce. Sprinkle with breadcrumbs and put on a few knobs of butter.
8. Heat for 15 minutes in the oven and serve immediately.

Asperges Gratinées au Jambon

Serves 6. Preparation and cooking: 50 min

Asparagus Gratin with Ham

★★

○ **1.5kg (3¼ lb) thin green asparagus**
○ **50g (2 oz) butter**
○ **30ml (2 tbls) flour**
○ **250ml (10 fl oz) milk**
○ **2 egg yolks**
○ **100g (4 oz) grated Gruyère cheese**
○ **100ml (3½ fl oz) dry white wine**
○ **6 slices cooked ham**
○ **15ml (1 tbls) coarse salt**
○ **salt and pepper**
○ **pinch nutmeg**

1. Place a large saucepan, three-quarters full of water, over a high heat, and add 15ml (1 tbls) coarse salt.
2. Scrape or peel, and wash asparagus. Cut into equal lengths and tie into 3 bundles.
3. When the water boils, place the bundles upright in the saucepan. The water should come to 1cm (½ inch) below asparagus tips to avoid spoiling them. Leave them in gently simmering water for about 20 minutes. They are cooked when the point of a knife pierces them easily.
4. Meanwhile, prepare the béchamel sauce. Melt the butter in a saucepan, gradually blend in the flour by mixing rapidly to avoid lumps. Pour in the milk all at once, stirring continuously. Bring to the boil and allow to cook for several minutes. Add salt, pepper, and nutmeg. Remove from heat, blend in the egg yolks, cheese and white wine. Leave to cool.
5. Set the oven at 230°C (450°F; gas mark 8).
6. When the asparagus is cooked, remove from water, untie, and drain on a rack. Divide into 6 small bundles and roll a slice of ham around each. Butter a gratin dish, arrange the parcels on it and sprinkle with béchamel sauce.
7. Put the dish in the oven for 10 minutes and serve very hot.

Asperges Sauce Gribiche

Serves 4. Preparation: 15 min Cooking: 20 min

Asparagus with Egg, Lemon and Herbs

★

○ **1kg (2¼ lb) asparagus**
○ **3 hard-boiled egg yolks**
○ **5ml (1 tsp) mustard**
○ **5ml (1 tsp) chopped capers**
○ **5ml (1 tsp) chopped herbs: parsley, chervil, tarragon**
○ **45ml (3 tbls) oil**
○ **juice of 1 lemon**
○ **15ml (1 tbls) coarse salt**
○ **salt and pepper**

1. Place a large saucepan, three-quarters full of water, on a high heat, and add coarse salt.
2. Scrape or peel, and wash asparagus. Cut the stalks to an equal length and tie up in a bundle.
3. When the water boils, place the bundle upright in the saucepan. The water should come 1cm (½ inch) below the tips so they do not get spoilt during cooking. Allow to simmer gently for about 20 minutes. They are cooked when the point of a knife pierces them easily.
4. Meanwhile, prepare the sauce. Place the egg yolks in a bowl and add the lemon juice, mustard and oil, mixing well, then add the capers, chopped herbs, salt and pepper.
5. When the asparagus is cooked, remove from water, untie and drain on a rack. Then arrange on a serving dish.
6. Serve the sauce in a sauceboat.

To clean asparagus stalks without causing any damage, place them flat on a table or a board and peel with a vegetable peeler from the tip towards the end. Always buy freshly picked stalks; their freshness is apparent on cutting. But on the other hand a fresh asparagus stalk breaks very easily and the juice will seep out.

Asperges Gratinées au Jambon ▶

Petit Sauté d'Aubergines

Serves 4. Preparation: 35 min Cooking: 40 min

Sautéed Aubergines

★

○ **3 large aubergines**
○ **3 medium potatoes**
○ **2 onions**
○ **2 ripe tomatoes**
○ **15ml (1 tbls) chopped parsley**
○ **60ml (4 tbls) oil**
○ **salt and pepper**

1. Wash the aubergines – do not peel them. Cut them into cubes 2cm (1 inch) square. Put cubes in a sieve, add salt and leave to drain for 30 minutes, then wash and wipe them.
2. Meanwhile peel the potatoes, wash them and cut into cubes 2cm (1 inch) square. Put these into cold water. Plunge the tomatoes into boiling water for 30 seconds, then strain them, place under cold running water and peel. Cut in two, remove the seeds, and chop roughly. Peel and mince the onions.
3. Heat some oil in a heavy pan, add all the vegetables and chopped parsley. Add salt and pepper. Cover. Cook for about 45 minutes turning from time to time.
4. Serve hot or completely cold and use as a garnish for roasts or grilled dishes.

Ratatouille Nicoise

Serves 2-4. Preparation: 15 min Cooking: 1 hr 15 min

Ratatouille (Aubergine, Pepper and Courgette Stew)

★ ★

○ **2 medium onions**
○ **2 large ripe tomatoes**
○ **2 peppers**
○ **2 courgettes**
○ **2 aubergines**
○ **2 garlic cloves**
○ **200ml (7 fl oz) olive oil**
○ **salt**

1. Plunge tomatoes into boiling water for 30 seconds, then strain them, cool by holding under cold running water, and peel. Cut in two horizontally, press to remove seeds, and chop roughly. Put on one side. Peel and chop finely the garlic cloves and onions.
2. Wash and wipe the peppers. Cut into half lengthways and remove the stalk, seeds and fibres. Cut the flesh into thin strips 1cm (½ inch) by 3cm (1½ inches) long. Wash aubergines and courgettes, wipe and remove stems. Do not peel. Cut into half lengthways, then into cubes 1.5cm (1 inch) square for the aubergines and 1cm (½ inch) square for the courgettes.
3. Heat 100ml (3½ fl oz) oil in a heavy pan over medium heat, and cook the aubergine cubes without letting them brown. Remove with a slotted spoon and put aside. Do the same with the courgettes and peppers. Add more oil during cooking if necessary.
4. In the same pan, lightly brown the chopped onions then add the tomatoes, chopped garlic, and the lightly cooked vegetables. If they are still coated in oil, do not add more to the pan. Add salt. Cover and leave to simmer gently, turning occasionally, for about 1 hour.
5. At the end of this time, the vegetables should be very tender, and only a little liquid should remain in the pan. If this is not the case continue cooking without the lid for a few minutes.

Hot or cold, ratatouille is a dish in its own right or an accompaniment to all roast meat, grilled or poached fish and eggs. Add a sprig of fresh basil in season. Ratatouille is traditionally cooked in a glazed earthenware dish.

Ratatouille Sicilienne

Ratatouille Sicilian-Style

Serves 4. Preparation: 20 min Cooking: 50 min approx

★★

○ **3 aubergines**
○ **6 ripe tomatoes**
○ **2 red peppers**
○ **2 green peppers**
○ **2 large onions**
○ **50g (2 oz) pitted green olives**
○ **50g (2 oz) pitted black olives**
○ **1 garlic clove**
○ **75ml (5 tbls) oil**
○ **15ml (1 tbls) chopped parsley**
○ **salt and pepper**

1. Peel the onions and garlic and chop finely. Plunge the tomatoes into boiling water for 30 seconds, strain and hold them under cold running water, then peel. Cut them in half to remove seeds and chop roughly into cubes. Peel the aubergines, wash them and cut into cubes 2cm (1 inch) square. Wash peppers, cut in half lengthways, remove seeds and slice finely.
2. Heat the oil in a saucepan and lightly brown the garlic and onion. Then add the aubergines and peppers and seal them. Then add the tomatoes; season with salt and pepper. Cover the pan tightly and cook for 30 minutes over a low heat.
3. At the end of this time, slice the olives and add to the pan. Leave to simmer for 10 minutes with no lid, then sprinkle with parsley and serve hot or cold.

Caponata

Ratatouille with Celery and Olives

Serves 4. Preparation and cooking: 40 min

★

○ **4 aubergines**
○ **1 onion**
○ **2 sticks of celery**
○ **100g (4 oz) pitted green olives**
○ **100ml (3½ fl oz) wine vinegar**
○ **10ml (2 tsp) tomato concentrate**
○ **5ml (1 flat tsp) sugar**
○ **60ml (4 tbls) olive oil**
○ **salt and pepper**

1. Wash the aubergines; do not peel but cut into cubes 2cm (1 inch) square. Peel the onion and chop small. Clean and chop the celery. Slice the olives.
2. Heat some oil in a heavy pan and lightly brown the pieces of aubergine over a high heat, turning often. Remove from pan with a slotted spoon and put them on one side.
3. In the oil in which the aubergines were cooked lightly brown the onion and celery. Add the vinegar, sugar, tomato concentrate and olives. Mix well and return the aubergines to the pan. Add salt and pepper. Cook over a low heat for 10 minutes, then remove from heat.

Allow the ratatouille to cool and serve as a main course with slices of bread.

Jerusalem artichokes, rather neglected nowadays, make a delicious purée. Peel them, wash and cut into cubes, and cook in salted boiling milk. After about 20 minutes, check cooking by piercing with the point of a knife. When cooked, drain and put through a sieve or blender to make a purée. Add salt, pepper and a knob of butter. The same quantity of potato purée may be added to this purée. To accompany game and grilled or roasted white meat, make the purée into rissoles and fry, or else half cook in milk and for the remaining time simmer in cream or a white sauce prepared with milk from the cooking. With cold meats, serve the artichokes cold with a vinaigrette dressing or luke-warm, prepared like potatoes with oil.

Barquettes d'Aubergines

Serves 4. Preparation: 45 min Cooking: 20 min

Stuffed Aubergines with Cheese

★★

- ○ **4 aubergines, not too small**
- ○ **40g (1¾ oz) dried mushrooms (cèpes)**
- ○ **1 egg**
- ○ **2 small sausages**
- ○ **100g (4 oz) soft white cheese: goat's milk or Ricotta**
- ○ **30ml (2 tbls) grated Gruyère or Parmesan cheese**
- ○ **1 garlic clove, finely chopped**
- ○ **45ml (3 tbls) oil**
- ○ **4 slices cheese for grilling**
- ○ **salt and pepper**

1. Wash, but do not peel the aubergines. Cut in two lengthways and arrange in a sieve, sprinkling salt between each layer of aubergines. Leave to drain for 30 minutes. Put mushrooms to soak in warm water.
2. At the end of this time, wash and wipe aubergines. Scoop out pulp and put on one side. Blanch aubergine shells for 5 minutes in salted boiling water. Strain.
3. Strain the mushrooms and chop finely. Skin the sausages and mash with a fork.
4. Mix the mushrooms and aubergine pulp with a fork in a dish. Add the chopped garlic, sausagemeat, soft white cheese and Gruyère cheese and beat in the egg. Add salt and pepper.
5. Set oven at 220°C (425°F; gas mark 7). Grease a gratin dish. Cut the grilling cheese in strips.
6. Stuff the aubergine shells and cover with cheese. Cook in oven for about 20 minutes until the cheese is golden brown. Serve very hot.

Gâteau de Légumes à l'Origan

Serves 4-6. Preparation: 10 min
Cooking: 1 hr 15 min

Vegetable Cake with Marjoram

★★

- ○ **4 large aubergines**
- ○ **4 large courgettes**
- ○ **5 large ripe tomatoes**
- ○ **12 leaves fresh basil**
- ○ **5ml (1 tsp) marjoram**
- ○ **salt and pepper**
- ○ **200ml (7 fl oz) olive oil for frying**

1. Peel aubergines. Cut them into slices ½cm (⅛ inch) thick, lengthways. Wash courgettes and wipe them. Do not peel. Cut them like the aubergines. Wash tomatoes. Cut into slices ½cm (⅛ inch) thick.
2. Heat 100ml (3½ fl oz) olive oil in large frying pan and fry the slices of courgettes very lightly without allowing to brown, then the slices of aubergines. Let them drain on kitchen paper.
3. Set the oven at 195°C (375°F; gas mark 5). Lightly grease base and sides of a medium-sized casserole about 22cm (10 inches) in diameter. Put a layer of tomatoes on the bottom, then a layer of courgettes, then a layer of aubergines. Continue in this fashion until all the vegetables are used up. Finish with a layer of tomatoes. Put the basil leaves between each layer, sprinkle with marjoram and add salt and pepper.
4. Cover the pan and cook in oven for 1 hour. Then remove, take off lid and wait for 5 minutes before turning the 'cake' out on to a serving dish. Serve either hot or cold.

This delicious savoury dish can be used as a main course or as an accompaniment for roasts, especially roast lamb or roast pork.

When buying courgettes, avoid those that are very dark green as they will be tasteless. If they are too big, they will have too many seeds. Choose smallish courgettes that are firm and shiny and never, never peel them before cooking or you will lose the best part of the vegetable.

Aubergines à la Parmesane

Serves 4. Preparation and cooking: 1 hr 50 min

Aubergines with Parmesan Cheese

★★

- ○ 1kg (2¼ lb) aubergines
- ○ 1kg (2¼ lb) ripe tomatoes
- ○ 300g (11 oz) Mozzarella cheese
- ○ 100g (4 oz) grated Parmesan cheese
- ○ 1 large onion
- ○ 1 garlic clove
- ○ 45ml (3 tbls) olive oil
- ○ groundnut oil for frying
- ○ salt and pepper

1. Wash aubergines, but do not peel them. Cut them lengthways into slices 1cm (½ inch) thick. Put them in a sieve with salt on each layer. Leave to drain for 1 hour.
2. Meanwhile, plunge the tomatoes into boiling water for 30 seconds. Drain them, then hold under cold running water. Peel tomatoes, cut in half, squeezing to remove the seeds, and chop coarsely.
3. Peel the onion and garlic and chop finely. Heat some olive oil in a frying pan and lightly brown the garlic and onion. Add the tomato. Add salt and pepper. Cook the sauce for 30 minutes, turning often.
4. Wash the aubergines, drain and dry with a cloth. Heat 90ml (6 tbls) groundnut oil in a large frying pan and lightly brown the aubergine slices on both sides. Drain them on kitchen paper. Add oil as needed during cooking.
5. Set oven at 220°C (425°F; gas mark 7).
6. Slice the Mozzarella thinly. Pour a little tomato sauce into the bottom of a high-sided ovenproof dish, then add a layer of aubergines, more tomato sauce, grated Parmesan cheese and finally a layer of Mozzarella. Continue like this until all the ingredients have been used up, finishing with a layer of tomato sprinkled with Parmesan cheese.
7. Cover the dish with foil and place in the oven for 30 minutes. Then remove the foil and cook uncovered for a further 10 minutes. Serve hot in the dish.

Aubergines en Beignets

Serves 4. Preparation: 2 hr 20 min Cooking: 30 min approx

Aubergine Fritters

★★★

- ○ 6 small round aubergines
- ○ 300g (11 oz) Gruyère or Gouda cheese
- ○ 60g (2½ oz) anchovy fillets, canned
- ○ 50g (2 oz) soft butter
- ○ 10 sprigs parsley
- ○ 6 leaves basil
- ○ 50g (2 oz) flour
- ○ 2 eggs
- ○ 45ml (3 tbls) breadcrumbs
- ○ oil for frying
- ○ salt and pepper

1. Wash but do not peel the aubergines. Cut them into slices widthways, 1cm (½ inch) thick. Arrange the slices in a sieve putting salt between each layer. Leave to drain for 2 hours.
2. At the end of this time, wash and wipe the aubergines. Slice the cheese thinly. Chop the herbs and mix with butter. Add salt and pepper.
3. On one slice of aubergine put a slice of cheese and an anchovy fillet. On another, spread some of the herb butter. Stick the two slices together, pressing firmly. Continue like this until all the ingredients are used up.
4. Beat the eggs well in a dish. Add the salt. Put the breadcrumbs and flour on two separate plates. Dip each aubergine 'sandwich', first in the flour, then in the egg and finally in the breadcrumbs.
5. Heat the oil in a frying pan and lightly brown the aubergine fritters over a medium heat for about 5 minutes on each side. Drain them on kitchen paper and keep them warm until all the fritters have been cooked. Serve hot.

Côtes de Blettes au Gratin

Serves 4. Preparation: 20 min cooking: 45 min

Seakale Gratin

★★

- ○ **1kg (2¼ lb) seakale**
- ○ **200g (7 oz) fresh cream**
- ○ **100g (4 oz) grated Gruyère cheese**
- ○ **1 egg**
- ○ **30g (1¼ oz) butter**
- ○ **juice of 1 lemon**
- ○ **salt and pepper**
- ○ **pinch nutmeg**

1. For this recipe, use only the white part (the ribs) of the seakale stalks. The leaves are delicious so put them aside for another dish. Cut the stalks into pieces 5cm-6cm (2-2½ inches) long, removing the vein and membrane which cover them.
2. Boil some water in a large saucepan, add salt and lemon juice, and blanch the seakale by gently simmering for 15 minutes, then strain.
3. Set the oven at 195°C (375°F; gas mark 5). Beat the egg well in a bowl and add the cream and cheese. Add salt, pepper and nutmeg. Mix well. Butter a gratin dish deep enough to hold two layers of the stalks one on top of the other. Lay half of them on the bottom; pour over half the egg, cream and cheese mixture; then make a second layer of seakale and cover with the remaining cream mixture.
4. Put the dish in the oven for 30 minutes. If after this time the top is not sufficiently golden, put it under a hot grill for 5 minutes. Serve very hot in the cooking dish.

This seakale gratin makes a very delicate accompaniment for all roast white meat.

Céleri-rave au Citron

Serves 4. Preparation and cooking: 40 min

Celeriac with Lemon

★★

- ○ **1 celeriac, about 600g (1¼ lb)**
- ○ **2 egg yolks**
- ○ **juice of 1 lemon**
- ○ **1 concentrated stock cube**
- ○ **250ml (9 fl oz) boiling water**
- ○ **50g (2 oz) butter**
- ○ **salt and pepper**

1. Peel, wash and quarter the celeriac, then cut into slices 1cm (½ inch) thick. Melt the butter in a frying pan and lightly brown the celeriac for 2 minutes on each side.
2. Dissolve the stock cube in boiling water and pour this into the pan. Add salt and pepper, and cover. Cook for 20 minutes over a gentle heat.
3. At the end of this time, put the celeriac into a serving dish, and continue simmering the cooking juices left in the pan over a very low heat. Beat the egg yolks in a bowl with the lemon juice and pour this mixture into the pan, beating continuously. Thicken the sauce for 1 minute and remove from heat.
4. Pour this sauce over the celeriac, and serve.

Seakale (or chard) is a wonderful vegetable with green leaves and white ribs or stalks. Each part is prepared differently and eaten separately. The leaves are excellent in stuffings and soups. Sharing the same qualities as spinach leaves, they can be prepared in similar ways. The ribs which were used in the above recipe can also be cooked in many ways. Here are two very simple recipes, which deserve to be more widely known. Blanch the seakale ribs, fry in butter with anchovy paste, then serve sprinkled with chopped parsley; or after blanching, cook them in a heavy pan with fresh cream. When the cream has reduced and the seakale is cooked, add crumbled Roquefort or Fourmé cheese. Mix well and serve when the cheese has melted. When the seakale is very young and the heads are not more than 25cm (12 inches) long, it is impossible to separate the leaves to cook them. So blanch them for 5 minutes, then fry them in butter or oil, or braise them with tomatoes and several cloves of garlic.

Coeurs de Céleri Braisés aux Olives

Serves 4. Preparation and cooking: 50 min

Braised Celery Hearts with Olives

★★

○ **8 small heads of celery**
○ **100g (4 oz) pitted black olives**
○ **500g (1 lb 2 oz) ripe tomatoes**
○ **2 peeled garlic cloves**
○ **15ml (1 tbls) chopped parsley**
○ **30ml (2 tbls) oil**
○ **50g (2 oz) butter**
○ **salt and pepper**

1. Discard the tough, outer stalks of the celery, and trim the leaves of the heart. Cut the hearts into 4. String with a sharp knife. Blanch them for 15 minutes in salted boiling water.
2. Meanwhile wash the tomatoes, quarter them and put them through a sieve or blender. Chop the olives. Strain the celery.
3. Heat the oil in a heavy pan, add the butter and lightly brown the garlic, then add the tomato purée, olives and parsley. Cook this mixture for 5 minutes on a medium heat and add the celery hearts, turning them with a wooden spoon so that they absorb the sauce. Add salt and pepper. Cover, and leave to simmer for 20 minutes over a low heat.
4. At the end of this time the celery should be tender and the sauce have greatly reduced. If it has not, cook uncovered for a few more minutes over a higher heat.
5. Arrange the celery in a dish, and serve hot.

Purée de Céleri-Rave

Serves 4-6. Preparation and cooking: 50 min

Purée of Celeriac

★★

○ **2 large celeriac roots**
○ **300g (11 oz) potatoes**
○ **100g (4 oz) fresh cream**
○ **50g (2 oz) butter**
○ **juice of 1 lemon plus ½ lemon**
○ **15ml (1 tbls) flour**
○ **salt and pepper**
○ **pinch nutmeg**

1. Peel the celeriac roots, quarter and squeeze lemon juice over the pieces to prevent discoloration. Leave to soak in cold water.
2. Bring some water to boil in a large saucepan. Add the salt, flour and lemon juice and gently simmer for 35 minutes.
3. Wash, peel, and quarter the potatoes and put them in the pan with the celeriac. After 35 minutes, check by piercing with a fork to see if the celeriac and potatoes are ready.
4. When the vegetables are cooked, strain them and put through a sieve or blender. Put the purée into a saucepan, add the cream and mix with a whisk. Add salt, pepper and nutmeg. Add butter and serve immediately, or keep warm until later.

This delicious purée can accompany all roasts and is especially good with game. A handful of chopped sorrel lightly browned in butter may be added.

When braising vegetables such as cabbage, celery hearts, leeks, or chicory they should first be blanched. This aids the cooking and helps to remove bitterness. They can then be braised in a slow oven or over a low heat by the following method. Grease a thick-bottomed pan generously with butter and put in a layer of sliced carrot and onion if you like. Arrange the vegetable to be braised on top and cover a quarter of the way up with stock. Add salt and pepper. Put in a few knobs of butter and cover. When they are cooked, strain the vegetables and arrange on a serving dish. Quickly reduce the cooking liquid, pour the residue over the vegetables, and serve. You may stuff such vegetables first, and cover the base of the pan with squares of pork fat or slices of lean bacon.

Aubergines à la Parmesane (p20) ▶

Carottes au Gruyère Filé

Serves 4. Preparation: 10 min Cooking: 40 min approx

Carrots with Gruyère Cheese

★

○ **800g (1¾ lb) new carrots**
○ **250g (9 oz) fresh cream**
○ **150g (6 oz) grated Gruyère cheese**
○ **50g (2 oz) butter**
○ **salt**

1. Peel and wash the carrots. Cut them into rounds 0.5cm (¼ inch) thick.
2. Melt the butter in a pan over a low heat and lightly brown the carrots; then add the fresh cream. Add salt. Cover the pan and cook over a low heat for about 30 minutes until all the liquid has disappeared.
3. Scatter the Gruyère over the carrots and mix everything together well so that the cheese melts equally. Serve very hot while the cheese is still runny.

Carottes et Pommes de Terre en Purée

Serves 4.
Preparation and cooking: 1 hr

Purée of Carrots and Potatoes

★★

○ **1kg (2¼ lb) carrots**
○ **300g (12 oz) potatoes**
○ **70g (3 oz) butter**
○ **50g (2 oz) grated Parmesan cheese or Gruyère cheese**
○ **200g (8 oz) fresh cream**
○ **1 onion, chopped small**
○ **salt and pepper**

1. Peel and wash the carrots. If the carrots are new leave them whole. If old, cut into cubes. Cook in boiling salted water for about 40 minutes.
2. Meanwhile, peel and wash the potatoes and put them into cold salted water. bring to the boil and cook gently for about 20 minutes.
3. When cooked, strain and put through a sieve or blender. Put the purée on one side.
4. Melt half the butter in a heavy pan. Add the chopped onion and brown lightly over a low heat. Add the purée to the pan and cook for 5 minutes turning continuously. Add the cheese and fresh cream. Season if necessary. Allow to simmer for 5 minutes, stirring well.

Serve this purée hot as an accompaniment to boiled or grilled meat.

Carottes Aigre-Douces

Serves 4. Preparation and cooking: 40 min

Sweet and Sour Carrots

★

○ **1kg (2¼ lb) new carrots**
○ **100g (4 oz) butter**
○ **250g (10 oz) fresh cream**
○ **5ml (1 tsp) sugar**
○ **juice of 1 lemon**
○ **salt**

1. Peel and wash the carrots. Cook in boiling, salted water for 10 minutes. Strain and cut into rounds 1cm (½ inch) thick.
2. Melt the butter in a frying pan, add carrots and brown lightly. Add sugar and stir continuously to caramelize the carrots. Add fresh cream. Leave to cook for 10 minutes over a very low heat.
3. At the end of this time, pour in lemon juice and mix together well. Serve hot.

These carrots are an excellent accompaniment to boiled meat.

Here is the simplest way to glaze carrots, turnips and whole onions as an accompaniment to meat and game. Peel the vegetables and place in a frying pan with a large lump of butter, salt and 5ml (1 tsp) of granulated sugar. Pour on water up to a quarter of their height and cook uncovered over a low heat until no liquid remains in the pan apart from a thick, syrup-like sauce. Turn the vegetables in this sauce until they are smooth and shiny.

Carottes aux Raisins de Smyrne

Serves 4. Preparation: 10 min Cooking: 1 hr

Carrots with Sultanas

★

- ○ **600g (1 lb 5 oz) new carrots**
- ○ **300g (11 oz) small new onions**
- ○ **150g (6 oz) sultanas**
- ○ **60g (2½ oz) butter**
- ○ **250ml (9 fl oz) white wine**
- ○ **100g (4 oz) cream**
- ○ **1 bay leaf**
- ○ **1 sprig thyme**
- ○ **salt and pepper**
- ○ **pinch cayenne pepper**

1. Wash the sultanas and leave to soak in cold water.
2. Peel and wash the carrots and onions. Drain the sultanas.
3. Melt the butter in a heavy pan and lightly brown the carrots and onions. Add salt, pepper, a pinch of cayenne pepper, the crushed thyme, bay leaf and sultanas. Cover with white wine and leave to cook covered over a very low heat for 45 minutes. Add fresh cream and mix together well. Cook for a further 10 minutes and serve immediately.

The sultanas may be replaced by muscatels. To give this dish a bitter-sweet flavour, substitute an equal amount of water and cider vinegar for the white wine.

Purée de Carottes au Lait

Serves 4. Preparation and cooking: 1 hr

Purée of Carrots with Milk

★

- ○ **1kg (2¼ lb) carrots**
- ○ **½ litre (18 fl oz) milk**
- ○ **6 green peppercorns**
- ○ **salt and pepper**
- ○ **pinch nutmeg**

1. Peel, wash and dice the carrots. Put into a saucepan and cover with milk. Add salt, nutmeg and green peppercorns.
2. Cook without a lid for 35 to 40 minutes until all the milk has evaporated. Remove from the heat, leave to cool, and then put the contents of the saucepan through a blender.
3. Reheat the purée over a very low heat, turning with a wooden spoon to prevent the bottom from scorching, and serve.

This purée may be served alone or with other vegetable purées to accompany white meat or poultry.

Soupe Paysanne

Serves 4. Preparation: 15 min Cooking: 40 min

Peasant-Style Soup

★★

- ○ **6 large carrots**
- ○ **4 small potatoes**
- ○ **2 large onions**
- ○ **2 turnips**
- ○ **3 leeks**
- ○ **1 celeriac**
- ○ **1 packet frozen peas**
- ○ **1 stock cube**
- ○ **¾ litre (27 fl oz) hot water**
- ○ **15ml (1 tbls) oil**
- ○ **20g (1 oz) butter**
- ○ **salt and pepper**

1. Peel and wash the carrots and cut into circles 1cm (½ inch) thick. Peel the onions and chop roughly. Wash and dice the celeriac and turnips.
2. Pour the oil into a large saucepan and add the carrots, onions, celeriac and turnips. Brown lightly.
3. Dissolve the stock cube in hot water. Pour into the pan and bring to the boil.
4. Peel, wash and quarter the potatoes. Peel and wash the leeks, and slice across finely. Place in pan with other vegetables and cook gently for 20 minutes.
5. At the end of this time, add the peas and simmer for another 15 minutes. Add the salt and pepper.
6. Stir in butter and serve hot.

Courgettes au Gratin

Serves 4. Preparation and cooking: 50 min approx

Gratin of Courgettes

★★

○ **1kg (2¼ lb) courgettes**
○ **500g (1 lb 2 oz) ripe tomatoes**
○ **150g (6 oz) grated Parmesan cheese**
○ **150g (6 oz) Gruyère cheese**
○ **30g (1¼ oz) flour**
○ **5ml (1 tsp) marjoram**
○ **45ml (3 tbls) olive oil**
○ **oil for frying**
○ **salt**

1. Cut off both ends of the courgettes. Wash and cut them lengthways into slices 1cm (½ inch) thick. Dip them in flour.
2. Heat oil in frying pan and lightly brown the courgette slices on both sides. Drain them on kitchen paper and add salt.
3. Wash tomatoes and pass them through a fine sieve or purée in the blender. Slice cheese finely.
4. Set oven at 220°C (425°F; gas mark 7).
5. Pour 30ml (2 tbls) olive oil in deep soufflé dish, then put a layer of fried courgettes, a layer of cheese and a layer of tomato purée. Add salt and marjoram. Continue thus until all the vegetables have been used up, finishing with a layer of tomato purée. Sprinkle the top with a spoonful of olive oil, and finish with Parmesan cheese.
6. Put the dish in the oven for 20 minutes and serve very hot.

Courgettes Farcies au Thon

Serves 4. Preparation: 20 min Cooking: 45 min

Courgettes Stuffed with Tuna

★★

○ **6 courgettes**
○ **1 tin 125g (4 oz) tuna**
○ **50g (2 oz) grated Gruyère cheese**
○ **15ml (1 tbls) chopped parsley**
○ **1 peeled garlic clove**
○ **1 egg**
○ **15ml (1 tbls) breadcrumbs**
○ **15ml (1 tbls) fresh cream**
○ **15ml (1 tbls) oil**
○ **200ml (7 fl oz) water**
○ **20g (1 oz) butter**
○ **salt and pepper**
○ **pinch nutmeg**

1. Cut off both ends of the courgettes, wash, but do not peel them. Cut in two lengthways. Hollow out the centre. Chop the flesh and put on one side.
2. Prepare the stuffing. Mash the tuna fish with a fork. Chop the garlic finely. Put these in a bowl with the courgette flesh, cheese, garlic and parsley and mix. Add cream and bind everything together with the egg. Season with salt, pepper and nutmeg. Mix again and stuff the courgette shells.
3. Set oven at 205°C (400°F; gas mark 6).
4. Oil an oven dish and arrange the courgettes in it. Scatter with breadcrumbs and dot with knobs of butter. Trickle the water round in the bottom of the dish.
5. Leave in the oven for 45 minutes. Add more water to the bottom of dish if necessary. Serve hot or cold.

Pepper is the most familiar of all the spices. In various forms – black or white, as whole peppercorns or crushed or milled – it is used as a seasoning to dishes the world over. Peppercorns are the dried fruit of the pepper plant. Black pepper, the unhusked seed, possesses an additional piquancy. White pepper, which has been 'shelled' and washed and has a less subtle flavour, has the advantage of being invisible in white sauces such as béchamel or mayonnaise. Green or fresh pepper is milder, more subtle, and altogether more exotic. It is sold loose and can also be found bottled, tinned, deep frozen or freeze dried. Loose it is rather tasteless, whereas deep frozen it is perhaps at its best, and in its freeze-dried form it can be used like black pepper. It is difficult to mill though, being too light, but is easily crushed with the fingers.

Mignonnette or steak pepper is a mixture of black and white pepper ground together. Intended first and foremost for steak, it is also used to season oysters and spicy sauces. Cayenne pepper is derived from the pimento and is extremely piquant.

Dôme de Courgettes

Serves 4. Preparation and cooking: 45 min approx

Courgettes with Veal

★ ★

- ○ **600g (1 lb 5 oz) courgettes**
- ○ **400g (14 oz) thinly beaten veal escalopes**
- ○ **80g (3¼ oz) butter**
- ○ **100g (4 oz) grated Gruyère cheese**
- ○ **salt and pepper**

1. Cut off both ends of the courgettes. Wash and cut into circles 0.5cm (⅛ inch) thick.
2. Melt half the butter in a frying pan and lightly brown the courgettes, turning them often with a wooden spoon. Add salt and pepper. Drain them in a colander and keep warm.
3. In the same pan melt the rest of the butter and cook the escalopes for 3 minutes on each side. Add salt and pepper. Deglaze the juices with 30ml (2 tbls) hot water.
4. Set oven to 220°C (425°F; gas mark 7).
5. Pour the deglazed juices into a round ovenproof dish and arrange a layer of courgettes in it, topped by a layer of cheese and a layer of escalopes. Continue in this way, building a dome, until all the ingredients have been used up, finishing with a layer of courgettes. Put in the oven for 15 minutes and serve immediately.

Cardons au Gratin

Serves 4. Preparation and cooking: 1 hr 50 min

Gratin of Cardoons (type of Globe Artichoke)

★ ★

- ○ **1kg (2¼ lb) cardoons**
- ○ **100g (4 oz) butter**
- ○ **100g (4 oz) grated Gruyère cheese**
- ○ **juice of 1 lemon plus ½ lemon**
- ○ **15ml (1 tbls) flour**
- ○ **salt and pepper**

1. Take off tough outer stalks of the cardoons. Discard all other fibrous parts. Trim remaining stalks and cut into 8cm (3 inch) long segments. Rub with lemon juice and drop into cold water. Add lemon juice, 15ml (1 tbls) of flour and salt to a pan of water and bring to a boil. Cook the cardoons gently in this for 1 hour 30 minutes. Drain.
2. Melt 50g (2 oz) butter in a pan, add the cardoons and brown lightly. Add salt and pepper.
3. Set oven at 230°C (450°F; gas mark 8).
4. Butter a gratin dish and put in half the cardoons. Sprinkle with the grated Gruyère and dot with butter. Add the remaining cardoons and the rest of the Gruyère and butter.
5. Place in the oven for 5 minutes and serve hot.

The method of cooking au blanc *is used for certain vegetables like cardoons, seakale or artichoke hearts which discolour rapidly when peeled. Once prepared, you should immediately rub them with half a lemon and plunge them into cold water with lemon juice added. Leave them until you need to use them. Place together in a pan 20g (¾ oz) flour, 10g (½ oz) salt, 1 litre (1¾ pints) of water and lemon juice. Bring to the boil, stirring well, then add the vegetables and cook for the length of time desired. If you are serving the vegetables cold, allow them to cool in the liquor. The lemon juice and the flour will prevent them from discolouring, the first because of its acidity and the second because it allows an inpenetrable skin to form. Such vegetables, which turn black on contact with the air, may also blacken your hands when preparing them. You will find you can remove the marks by rubbing with half a lemon.*

Cardons à la Sauce aux Oeufs

Serves 4. Preparation and cooking: 1 hr 45 min

Cardoons with Egg Sauce

★★

- ○ **1kg (2¼ lb) cardoons**
- ○ **80g (3¼ oz) butter**
- ○ **30ml (2 tbls) flour**
- ○ **2 egg yolks**
- ○ **1 onion**
- ○ **juice of 2 lemons plus ½ lemon**
- ○ **1 stock cube**
- ○ **200ml (7 fl oz) hot water**
- ○ **salt**

1. Discard the tough, outer stalks and all the fibrous parts of the cardoons. Cut the remaining stalks into 5cm (2 inch) long segments, discarding the leaves. Rub the cardoons with the half lemon and put them into cold water.
2. Add the juice of one lemon and 15ml (1 tbls) of flour to water in a pan and bring to a boil. Cook the cardoons in this for 1 hour 30 minutes, simmering gently. The lemon and flour ensure that the vegetables remain white.
3. 15 minutes before the cardoons are cooked, peel and chop the onions finely. Prepare the stock by dissolving the cube in hot water. Melt half the butter in a saucepan and brown the onion lightly. Add the second 15ml (1 tbls) of flour and work well in. Pour in the stock gradually and cook for 10 minutes over a low heat.
4. In a bowl, beat the egg yolks well. Add the juice of the other lemon. Season with salt and add to the sauce. Cook for a further 5 minutes stirring all the time.
5. When the cardoons are cooked, strain them and brown them lightly in a pan with the remaining butter.
6. Arrange on a serving dish and trickle the sauce over. Serve hot.

Cardons à la Moelle

Serves 4. Preparation: 10 min Cooking: 1 hr 40 min approx

Cardoons with Beef Marrow

★★

- ○ **1kg (2¼ lb) cardoons**
- ○ **200g (8 oz) beef marrow**
- ○ **50g (2 oz) butter**
- ○ **juice of 1 lemon plus ½ lemon**
- ○ **15ml (1 tbls) flour**
- ○ **salt and pepper**

1. Discard the tough outer stalks and all the fibrous parts of the cardoons. Cut the remaining stalks into 5cm (2 inch) segments. Rub with lemon and put in cold water.
2. Add the flour and lemon juice to a pan of water and bring to the boil. Cook the cardoons in this for 1 hour 30 minutes, simmering gently.
3. When the cardoons are cooked, strain in a colander.
4. Add the beef marrow to boiling, salted water and poach for 10 minutes by simmering gently. Then remove with a slotted spoon, drain, and cut into thin discs.
5. Melt the butter in a frying pan and lightly brown the cardoons. Season with salt and pepper.
6. Arrange the cardoons on a serving dish and lay the sliced beef marrow on top. Serve very hot.

You can, if you like, arrange the cardoons in a gratin dish and cover with the slices of beef marrow. Sprinkle 50g (2 oz) grated Gruyère cheese over and put in a very hot oven for 5 minutes.

A note about breadcrumbs. Toasted breadcrumbs, used for gratin dishes, can be kept for a long time in a dry place. You make them by drying slices of stale bread very slowly in the oven and then crushing with a rolling pin. White breadcrumbs are used for frying. They are made from stale bread with the crusts removed which has been crushed with a rolling pin and then passed through a coarse sieve. Or you can make them in a food blender.

Cèpes à la Menthe

Serves 4. Preparation: 10 min Cooking: 45 min

Cèpes with Mint

★★

- ○ **500g (1 lb 2 oz) cèpes**
- ○ **2ml (½ tsp) thyme flowers**
- ○ **10 sprigs parsley**
- ○ **4 leaves fresh mint**
- ○ **2 peeled garlic cloves**
- ○ **100ml (3½ fl oz) dry white wine**
- ○ **15ml (1 tbls) fresh cream**
- ○ **45ml (3 tbls) oil**
- ○ **salt and pepper**

1. Clean the mushrooms without washing. Scrape stalks with a small knife and wipe the tops. Slice thinly.
2. Heat some oil in a pan. Add the mushrooms with the garlic cloves. Cook for 5 minutes over a high heat at first, then lower. Season with the salt, pepper and thyme. Sauté for 15 minutes.
3. Meanwhile, wash and wipe the parsley and mint and chop finely.
4. When the mushrooms have cooked for 15 minutes add the white wine and simmer until the liquid has completely evaporated, about 20 minutes.
5. Now sprinkle the parsley and mint over the mushrooms and add the cream. Reduce by cooking further before serving.

Cèpes prepared like this make the perfect accompaniment to roast lamb or game. Other chopped herbs may be used instead of mint.

Cèpes à la Bordelaise

Serves 3-4. Preparation: 15 min Cooking: 20 min approx

Cèpes with Shallots

★

- ○ **500g (1 lb 2 oz) cèpes**
- ○ **3 shallots**
- ○ **45ml (3 tbls) olive oil**
- ○ **50g (2 oz) stale bread**
- ○ **15ml (1 tbls) chopped parsley**
- ○ **½ lemon**
- ○ **salt and pepper**

1. Take off mushroom stalks, scrape with a paring knife, and chop into small pieces. Wipe tops and slice thinly. Do not mix.
2. Remove the bread crusts. Grate the bread – you will need 30ml (2 tbls). Peel and chop shallots finely.
3. Heat the oil in a frying pan over a high heat and throw in the sliced mushrooms. Sauté for about 15 minutes, turning frequently until the juices have run and the mushrooms are lightly browned. Then add the chopped stalks, shallots and breadcrumbs. Season with salt and pepper. Sauté together for 5 minutes more and remove from heat.
4. Arrange the mushrooms on a serving dish, sprinkle with parsley, squeeze lemon juice over and serve immediately.

Cèpes prepared in this way (*à la bordelaise*) go perfectly with grills and with braised or roasted game. The shallots may be replaced with garlic cloves, as they do in Provence.

Fennel, grown in the south of France and in Italy, is available from May to December. It may be eaten raw, finely sliced and dressed with a vinaigrette containing lemon juice. Or it may be added to other salads. Cooked fennel is a delicious accompaniment to all white meat and poultry. Be sure to blanch it first before cooking in butter or cream. Serve it sprinkled with herbs and grated cheese, or place under the grill to turn golden. The leaves of the best fennel are very green, and the bulb should be fleshy, round and very white.

Lovers of green vegetables who dislike the bitterness of spinach may like to learn of a ribless variety of seakale which resembles spinach in size and colour but has a sweet, very mild taste. It is becoming increasingly available as its popularity grows since, once tasted, you will want to try it again!

Dôme de Courgettes (p28) ▶

Chou Farci

Serves 6. Preparation: 30 min Cooking: 2 hr

Stuffed Cabbage

★★★

○ **1 large green cabbage, about 1.5kg (3¼ lb)**
○ **100g (4 oz) sausagemeat**
○ **100g (4 oz) smoked bacon**
○ **300g (11 oz) pickled pork**
○ **50g (2 oz) grated Gruyère cheese**
○ **100g (4 oz) white breadcrumbs or**
○ **200g (8 oz) cooked rice**
○ **1 egg**
○ **1 stock cube**
○ **½ litre (18 fl oz) hot water**
○ **1 garlic clove**
○ **15ml (1 tbls) chopped parsley**
○ **salt and pepper**

1. Take off any damaged leaves and wash the cabbage. Bring to the boil some water in a saucepan big enough to hold the cabbage and add salt; blanch by simmering for 15 minutes. Strain, pressing down well in the colander to eliminate all the water.
2. Meanwhile, prepare the stuffing: peel and chop the garlic finely. Dice the pork and bacon as small as possible. Mash the sausagemeat with a fork. Mix everything together in a bowl and add the breadcrumbs, grated cheese and chopped parsley. Bind together with an egg. Season and mix again.
3. Gently open out the leaves of the cabbage from the heart outwards. Place a spoonful of stuffing in the centre and spread another spoonful between each layer of leaves. Use up all the stuffing. Tie the cabbage with string like a parcel, leaving the knot at the top so that you will be able to lift it from the pan.
4. Set the oven at 195°C (375°F; gas mark 5). Dissolve the stock cube in hot water.
5. Put the cabbage in a pan and cover with stock, adding more water if necessary. Bring to the boil over a high heat. Cover and place in the oven for 2 hours.
6. Remove the cabbage from the stock by the knot, then cut the thread. Place on a serving dish, pour the stock into a sauceboat, and serve.

Boiled or puréed potatoes make the perfect accompaniment to this dish.

Feuilles de Chou Farcies

Serves 4. Preparation: 30 min Cooking: 50 min

Stuffed Cabbage Leaves

★★★

○ **8 undamaged green cabbage leaves**
○ **100g (4 oz) sausagemeat**
○ **100g (4 oz) cooked ham**
○ **2 eggs**
○ **100g (4 oz) grated Gruyère cheese**
○ **100ml (3½ fl oz) milk**
○ **50g (2 oz) bread without crusts**
○ **60g (2½ oz) butter**
○ **salt and pepper**
○ **pinch nutmeg**
○ **1 tin (14 oz) peeled tomatoes (optional)**

1. Wash the cabbage leaves. Blanch in boiling, salted water for 3 minutes, cool under a running tap and drain. Place on a cloth.
2. Crumble the bread and soak it in milk.
3. Chop the ham as small as possible and mash the sausagemeat. Mix together in a bowl. Add the eggs and the Gruyère cheese and mix again.
4. Squeeze out the bread and mix with the stuffing. Add salt, pepper and nutmeg. Work well with a fork.
5. Put a little stuffing in each cabbage leaf. Fold the leaf in four and tie up with kitchen thread.
6. Purée the tinned tomatoes through a sieve or blender.
7. Melt the butter in a heavy pan. Add the cabbage parcels and lightly brown all over. Then add the tomato purée, salt, pepper and nutmeg. Cover the pan. Leave to cook for 45 minutes over a low heat turning the stuffed leaves once. Serve either hot or cold.

You may replace the tomato purée with 250ml (9 fl oz) beef or chicken stock.

Chou au Vinaigre

Serves 4. Preparation: 15 min Cooking: 40 min

Cabbage in Vinegar

★

- ○ **1 cabbage or kale about 1kg (2¼ lb)**
- ○ **50g (2 oz) smoked bacon**
- ○ **1 peeled garlic clove**
- ○ **30ml (2 tbls) oil**
- ○ **100ml (3½ fl oz) vinegar**
- ○ **100ml (3½ fl oz) water**
- ○ **salt and pepper**

1. Take off the stem and any damaged leaves and cut the cabbage into four. Wash, then chop finely. Blanch the cabbage for 5 minutes in a large quantity of boiling, salted water and strain.
2. Dice the bacon.
3. Heat the oil in a large pan and lightly brown the whole garlic clove and the bacon. Add the cabbage and cook for 5 minutes, turning often. Pour in the water and vinegar, and season. Cover and cook for 25 minutes over a low heat, turning now and then. At the end of this time if any liquid is left in the pan reduce by cooking uncovered over a high heat for 5 minutes more.

Served very hot, this cabbage can accompany goose, duck, and all kinds of pork dishes, whether grilled or roasted.

Chou Braisé à la Tomate

Serves 4. Preparation: 10 min Cooking: 40 min

Braised Cabbage with Tomato

★

- ○ **1 cabbage or kale about 800g (1¾ lb)**
- ○ **100g (4 oz) smoked bacon**
- ○ **6 ripe plum tomatoes**
- ○ **2 peeled garlic cloves**
- ○ **60ml (4 tbls) oil**
- ○ **salt and pepper**

1. Take off the stem and any damaged leaves and cut the cabbage into four. Chop well. Cut the bacon into sticks 0.5cm (¼ inch) thick.
2. Heat the oil in a pan and lightly brown the bacon and garlic. Then remove the garlic and add the cabbage. Mix well with the bacon, add salt and pepper and cover. Leave to cook for 10 minutes over a low heat.
3. Meanwhile, plunge the tomatoes into boiling water for 30 seconds. Drain and cool under a running tap. Peel, cut in half to remove the seeds, and chop roughly.
4. Add the tomatoes to the pan and stir in well. Cover again and leave to cook for a further 25 minutes.

Serve hot to accompany braised or roast pork, frankfurters, or grilled sausages, etc.

Choux de Bruxelles à la Crème

Serves 4. Preparation and cooking: 35 min

Brussels Sprouts with Cream

★★

- ○ **800g (1¾ lb) Brussels sprouts**
- ○ **300g (11 oz) fresh cream**
- ○ **1 onion, chopped small**
- ○ **60g (2 oz) flour**
- ○ **15ml (1 tbls) flour**
- ○ **salt and pepper**

1. Wash and drain the sprouts, discarding the outer leaves. Cook for 15 to 20 minutes in boiling, salted water, until they are tender.
2. Melt 50g (2 oz) butter in a pan and lightly brown the chopped onion. Add the sprouts and sauté gently, adding salt and pepper. Pour in half the fresh cream. Stir well and cook for 10 minutes over a low heat.
3. Pour the other half of the cream into a saucepan, together with the remaining butter and flour. Beat with a whisk and cook for 5 minutes. Pour this sauce over the sprouts. Serve.

You may garnish this dish with gherkins and other small pickles.

Chou-Fleur Froid aux Langoustines

Serves 4. Preparation and cooking: 1 hr

Cold Cauliflower with Scampi

★★

○ **1 large cauliflower**
○ **12 scampi**

For the stock:
○ **2 litres (3½ pints) cold water**
○ **1 litre (1¾ pints) dry white wine**
○ **100ml (3½ fl oz) vinegar**
○ **40g (2 oz) sea salt**
○ **2 carrots**
○ **1 medium-sized onion**
○ **10 peppercorns**
○ **2 cloves**
○ **1 bouquet garni consisting of: 10 sprigs parsley, 1 sprig thyme and 1 bay leaf**

For the sauce:
○ **250ml (9 fl oz) oil**
○ **2 egg yolks**
○ **5ml (1 tsp) mustard**
○ **juice of 1 lemon**
○ **100ml (3½ fl oz) fresh cream**
○ **salt**
○ **pinch curry powder**

1. Wash the cauliflower. Cook for 15 minutes by simmering gently, head downwards, in boiling salted water. Drain.
2. Meanwhile, prepare the court-bouillon. Peel and wash the carrots. Peel onion and spike with cloves. Put the water, wine, vinegar, onion, carrots, bouquet garni and pepper into a large saucepan. Bring to the boil, add salt and boil for 30 minutes. Then add the scampi. Cook for a further 5 minutes, turn off the heat, and allow to cool in the court-bouillon before straining.
3. Prepare the sauce. Put the egg yolks, salt, mustard and lemon juice into a bowl. Beat quickly with a whisk. Dribble the oil in slowly, beating all the time. When the mayonnaise is ready, fold in the fresh cream. Mix. Pour the sauce into a sauceboat and add a pinch of curry powder.
4. Place the cauliflower on a serving dish, and trickle a little sauce over. Surround with the scampi. The remaining sauce should be served separately.

You can enrich this dish with hard-boiled eggs and cold artichoke hearts. The scampi may be replaced by all kinds of shellfish: shrimps, king prawns, or crabs.

Chou-Fleur aux Deux Paprikas

Serves 4. Preparation and cooking: 40 min

Cauliflower with Two Kinds of Paprika

★★

○ **1 large cauliflower**
○ **100g (4 oz) bacon**
○ **150g (6 oz) button mushrooms**
○ **150g (6 oz) fresh cream**
○ **60g (2½ oz) butter**
○ **10 chives**
○ **50g (2 oz) grated Gruyère cheese**
○ **5ml (1 tsp) mild paprika**
○ **5ml (1 tsp) strong paprika**
○ **salt and pepper**

1. Wash the cauliflower and separate it into individual flowerets. Cook for about 10 minutes in boiling salted water. Do not let them become mushy. Strain.
2. Meanwhile, cut the bacon into strips. Trim, wipe and slice the mushrooms.
3. Melt 40g (1¼ oz) butter in a heavy pan and sauté the bacon and mushrooms. Season with salt and pepper and the strong paprika. Add the cauliflower flowerets and brown them lightly, turning carefully.
4. Set the oven at 220°C (425°F; gas mark 7). Grease a gratin dish with the remaining butter and pour in the contents of the pan. Cover with fresh cream and the grated cheese and cook in the oven for 10 minutes.
5. Meanwhile, chop the chives. When the dish is cooked, garnish with the chives and the mild paprika. Serve immediately.

The button mushrooms may be replaced by flat-topped mushrooms, or any wild variety.

To make what the French call potatoes au diable you need a special covered dish made of porous clay. Known as a 'devil', it consists of two vessels which fit into each other and is turned over during cooking, which is done over direct heat. The inside of the 'devil' is rubbed with garlic, and the potatoes are baked in their jackets with a sprig of thyme or rosemary and some bay leaves. They are eaten with butter or cream. The variety of potato most suited to this method of cooking is a particularly early kind known as Early Rose.

Chou aux Herbes à l'Italienne

Serves 4. Preparation: 10 min Cooking: 1 hr 10 min

Cabbage with Herbs, Italian-Style

★★

○ **1 large green cabbage**
○ **2 well chopped onions**
○ **30g (1¼ oz) butter**
○ **150g (6 oz) smoked bacon**
○ **200ml (7 fl oz) oil**
○ **1 sprig rosemary**
○ **4 sage leaves**
○ **6 basil leaves**
○ **1 tin (14 oz) peeled tomatoes**
○ **1 stock cube**
○ **100ml (3½ fl oz) hot water**
○ **salt and pepper**

1. Take off the stem and any damaged leaves, and quarter the cabbage. Wash and slice finely. Chop the bacon into sticks.
2. Put the oil in a heavy pan, add the butter, and brown the onions lightly. Add the bacon, rosemary, basil and sage. When the bacon has browned, add the cabbage.
3. Mash the tinned tomatoes roughly with a fork and pour them with their juice into the pan. Then dissolve the stock cube in hot water and pour in pan as well. Add salt and pepper. Cover the pan and leave to simmer for 1 hour over a gentle heat.
4. Remove the herbs to serve. Reduce the liquor as much as possible by bring to a boil, uncovered.

Serve this flavoursome dish with frankfurters or cold pickled pork.

Chou Rouge à la Flamande

Serves 4. Preparation and cooking: 1 hr

Flemish Red Cabbage

★★

○ **1 small red cabbage**
○ **1 small white cabbage**
○ **150g (6 oz) lean bacon**
○ **2 apples**
○ **60g (2½ oz) butter**
○ **salt and pepper**

1. Take off the stems and any damaged leaves and wash both cabbages. Cook the cabbages separately for 15 minutes in boiling salted water. Strain and leave to cool. Separate the leaves.
2. Take two red leaves and roll them up tightly. Do the same with two white leaves. Continue in this fashion until all the leaves are used up.
3. Set the oven at 220°C (425°F; gas mark 7). Grease a gratin dish with 20g (¾ oz) butter and arrange the cabbage rolls in it.
4. Peel the apples and cut into slices. Place a slice of apple on each roll of red cabbage. Cut the bacon into strips and place one on each roll of white cabbage. Finally, place a knob of butter on every roll. Put the dish into the oven for 20 minutes and serve very hot.

Purée de Chou-Fleur

Serves 4. Preparation and cooking: 40 min

Purée of Cauliflower

★

○ **1 large cauliflower**
○ **125g (4 oz) fresh cream**
○ **salt and pepper**

1. Wash the cauliflower and cut off the stalk. Steam for about 30 minutes, until it is very tender.
2. When it is cooked, strain and separate the flowerets. Put them through a sieve or blender.
3. Put the purée into a saucepan over a low heat and fold in the cream. Add the salt and pepper. Reduce the cream for 5 minutes, cooking uncovered. Serve immediately or keep warm.

Puréed cauliflower goes very well with all kinds of roast meat.

Chou-Fleur en Beignets

Serves 4. Preparation: 15 min Cooking: 30 min

Cauliflower Fritters

★★★

○ **1 large cauliflower**
○ **oil for frying**
○ **salt**

For the batter:
○ **250g (9 oz) flour**
○ **50g (2 oz) melted butter**
○ **2 eggs**
○ **200ml (7 fl oz) beer**
○ **200ml (7 fl oz) water or milk**
○ **2ml (½ tsp) fine salt**

1. First prepare the batter. In a bowl mix together the flour, salt and egg yolks. Dilute by adding the beer little by little, then add the water or the milk, and finally the melted butter. Beat well and leave the mixture to stand for two hours.
2. 15 minutes before this time has elapsed, wash the cauliflower and separate it into flowerets. Cook for about 10 minutes in boiling salted water, then strain.
3. Beat the egg whites until stiff and fold them into the batter. Put the flowerets into the batter.
4. Heat the oil in a frying pan. When it begins to smoke, slide some of the batter-coated flowerets into the pan. Brown well, remove with a slotted spoon or slice, and drain on kitchen paper. Keep warm. Continue with the rest of the batter.
5. When all the fritters are cooked, heap on a serving dish and serve immediately.

Chou-Fleur aux Amandes

Serves 4. Preparation and cooking: 30 min approx

Cauliflower with Almonds

★★

○ **1 large cauliflower**
○ **50g (2 oz) flaked almonds**
○ **50g (2 oz) butter**
○ **50g (2 oz) flour**
○ **250ml (9 fl oz) milk**
○ **125g (6 oz) fresh cream**
○ **2ml (½ tsp) sugar**
○ **juice of 1 lemon**
○ **salt and pepper**

1. Wash the cauliflower and separate it into large flowerets. Boil in salted water for about 20 minutes until they are tender.
2. Meanwhile, melt the butter in a saucepan and fold in the flour, turning rapidly. Pour in the milk, stirring all the time. Cook for 10 minutes. Then lower the heat and fold in the fresh cream. Add the salt and pepper, the sugar and the lemon juice. Allow the mixture to cook for a further 2 minutes. When the cauliflower is cooked, strain and arrange on a serving dish.
3. Put the almonds into a frying pan without any fat and cook them over a high heat. When they are browned, sprinkle over the cauliflower and then pour the sauce over. Serve hot.

Frying is an excellent method of cooking starchy vegetables like potatoes. As soon as it comes into contact with the hot oil the starch forms a protective film around the vegetables, letting the inside steam-cook in the evaporation of its own liquid. In this way, the vegetables are crisp outside and soft inside. Vegetables low in starch can be floured or coated in batter before being fried. But it is better not to flour some vegetables before sealing them in the frying pan. In the case of aubergines (when you are going to cook them with Parmesan cheese, for instance) you should simply cut them into thick slices and seal before baking in the oven. When they are fried the aubergine slices absorb a great deal of oil, but on being removed from the pan they give most of it out again. Put them in a sieve or place them on kitchen paper to drain thoroughly.

If you want to make a batter for raw vegetables, mix 250g (9 oz) flour, 50g (2 oz) melted butter and 2 whole eggs. Add water gradually until you have obtained a cream consistency. Leave it to stand for at least 1 hour before coating the vegetables and frying. If the vegetables have been previously blanched (cauliflowers, celery, fennel) make the batter thicker by adding the yolk of two eggs. Just before cooking, fold in the stiffly beaten egg whites.

Chou-Fleur au Gratin

Serves 4. Preparation and cooking: 35 min

Cauliflower Cheese

★★

○ **1 large cauliflower**
○ **50g (2 oz) flour**
○ **70g (3 oz) butter**
○ **½ litre (18 fl oz) milk**
○ **100g (4 oz) fresh cream**
○ **50g (2 oz) grated Gruyère cheese**
○ **salt and pepper**
○ **pinch nutmeg**

1. Wash the cauliflower and separate into small flowerets. Boil gently in salted water for 10 minutes.
2. Meanwhile, prepare the béchamel sauce. Melt 50g (2 oz) butter in a saucepan and blend in the flour gradually, stirring constantly to avoid any lumps. Pour in the milk slowly, stirring all the time. Bring to the boil and leave to cook for 5 minutes. Add salt, pepper and nutmeg. Remove from the heat and blend in the fresh cream.
3. Set oven at 230°C (450°F; gas mark 8).
4. Strain the cauliflower. Butter a gratin dish. Arrange the cauliflower on it and pour over the béchamel. Scatter with grated cheese and cook in the oven for 15 minutes before serving immediately.

Chou à l'Aigre-Doux

Serves 4. Preparation: 30 min Cooking: 1 hr approx

Sweet and Sour Cabbage

★★

○ **1 large white cabbage**
○ **1 large onion**
○ **50g (2 oz) smoked bacon**
○ **100ml (3½ fl oz) oil**
○ **50g (2 oz) butter**
○ **100ml (3½ fl oz) vinegar**
○ **1 stock cube**
○ **250ml (9 fl oz) hot water**
○ **5ml (1 tsp) sugar**
○ **salt and pepper**

1. Boil 2 litres (3½ pints) water.
2. Cut off the stalk and discard any damaged leaves. Quarter and slice the cabbage. Put in the boiling water and leave to get completely cool.
3. When cold, drain the cabbage carefully. Peel and chop the onion. Cut the bacon into sticks.
4. Put half the oil and half the butter into a heavy pan. Lightly brown the onion in it, together with the bacon. Add the cabbage, then the salt and pepper.
5. Dissolve the stock cube in hot water and pour into the pan. Cook over a low heat uncovered for about 20 minutes until no stock is left. Then add the rest of the oil and the butter, the vinegar and the sugar. Mix well. Cover and cook for a further 40 minutes over a low heat. If there is any liquor left, reduce for a few minutes over a high heat, stirring continuously.

This cabbage dish makes an excellent accompaniment for goose and roast sucking pig.

Chou-Fleur Sauté

Serves 4. Preparation and cooking: 30 min

Sautéed Cauliflower with Onions and Sausagemeat

★

○ **1 large cauliflower**
○ **40g (1¾ oz) butter**
○ **2 medium-sized onions**
○ **100g (4 oz) sausagemeat**
○ **salt and pepper**

1. Wash the cauliflower and separate it into small flowerets.
2. Boil some water in a large saucepan, add salt and cook the cauliflower by simmering gently for 15 minutes.
3. Meanwhile, peel the onions and chop into small pieces.
4. Melt the butter in a frying pan and brown the onions lightly. Add the sausagemeat and brown it lightly, using a fork to break it up.
5. When the cauliflower is cooked, strain and add to the frying pan, stirring all together well. Season with pepper and serve.

Choux de Bruxelles au Jambon

Brussels Sprouts with Ham

*Serves 4. Preparation: 15 min
Cooking: 30 min approx*
★

○ **500g (1 lb 2 oz) Brussels sprouts**
○ **100g (4 oz) thin rashers smoked bacon**
○ **100g (4 oz) cooked ham**
○ **50g (2 oz) butter**
○ **1 stock cube**
○ **½ litre (18 fl oz) hot water**
○ **salt and pepper**
○ **pinch nutmeg**

1. Pull off the outer leaves, then wash the sprouts in lots of water and drain. Slice the ham finely. Butter an ovenproof dish, and line it, first with the bacon, then a layer of sprouts, another layer of bacon, a layer of sprouts. Top with the slices of ham.
2. Set the oven at 195°C (375°F; gas mark 5). Dissolve the stock cube in hot water and pour into the dish. Add salt, pepper and nutmeg.
3. Dot with butter and put in the oven. Cook for about 30 minutes until the sprouts are tender and the liquid has completely evaporated. Serve hot.

Chou au Fromage

Cabbage with Cheese Sauce

Serves 4. Preparation and cooking: 50 min approx
★★

○ **1 cabbage or kale about 1kg (2¼ lb)**
○ **50g (2 oz) lard**
○ **½ litre (18 fl oz) cold water**
○ **salt**

For the sauce:
○ **125g (6 oz) smoked bacon**
○ **125g (6 oz) grated Gruyère cheese**
○ **40g (2 oz) flour**
○ **1 medium-sized onion**
○ **salt and pepper**
○ **pinch nutmeg**

1. Cut off the stalk, discarding any withered leaves, and quarter the cabbage. Wash and slice it. Melt the lard in a pan, put in the cabbage and cook for 5 minutes over a low heat, stirring frequently. Then pour in the cold water, add the salt, and cook covered for 25 minutes over a low heat.
2. Meanwhile, prepare the sauce. Peel the onion and chop it finely. Cut the bacon into thin sticks and put them into a saucepan without any fat. Brown the bacon over a low heat. Add the onion, and when it is transparent, drench with the flour. Stir constantly until the flour has changed colour; then remove from the heat.
3. Strain the cabbage, then pour the stock it has cooked in into the saucepan. Add salt, pepper and nutmeg. Cook for 5 minutes over a medium heat, stirring constantly, then add the cheese, making sure it blends in well. When the sauce has thickened, add the cabbage. Cook everything for 3 minutes, and serve.

Flan d'Épinards

Baked Spinach with Eggs and Cream

Serves 4. Preparation: 20 min Cooking: 30 min
★★

○ **1kg (2¼ lb) spinach**
○ **4 eggs**
○ **60ml (4 tbls) fresh cream**
○ **15ml (1 tbls) white breadcrumbs**
○ **2 peeled garlic cloves**
○ **60ml (4 tbls) olive oil**
○ **40g (1¾ oz) butter**
○ **salt and pepper**
○ **pinch nutmeg**

1. Trim the spinach stalks, and wash and drain the leaves in a colander. Cut into broad segments.
2. Heat some oil in a frying pan and brown the garlic lightly. Add the spinach and salt and cook for 5 minutes, then remove from the heat and discard the garlic.
3. Beat the eggs well in a bowl with the fresh cream. Add salt, pepper and nutmeg. Pour onto the spinach and mix together well.
4. Set the oven at 212°C (412°F; gas mark 6½).
5. Grease a soufflé dish or mould with half the butter. Pour in the contents of the frying pan, scatter with breadcrumbs and dot with the remaining butter.
6. Place in the oven for 20 minutes and serve from the dish.

Gâteau d'Épinards
Spinach Cake

Serves 4. Preparation and cooking: 1 hr 15 min

★★★

○ **1kg (2¼ lb) spinach**
○ **15ml (1 tbls) coarse salt**
○ **30ml (2 tbls) fresh cream**
○ **30g (1¼ oz) butter**

For the sauce:
○ **1 tin 400g (14 oz) peeled tomatoes**
○ **1 carrot**
○ **1 stick celery**
○ **1 onion**
○ **100g (4 oz) shelled fresh peas**
○ **20g (1 oz) butter**
○ **15ml (1 tbls) oil**
○ **salt and pepper**

For the omelettes:
○ **4 eggs**
○ **50g (2 oz) grated Gruyère cheese**
○ **45ml (3 tbls) fresh cream**
○ **45ml (3 tbls) oil**
○ **salt and pepper**
○ **pinch nutmeg**

1. Clean and wash the spinach but do not drain. Put the moist leaves in a large saucepan and add the coarse salt. Cover and cook for 10 minutes in their own juice over a low heat.
2. Meanwhile, peel and slice the carrot thinly. Peel and chop the celery and onion.
3. Prepare the sauce. Pour the oil into a heavy pan, adding the butter, then the carrot, celery and onion. Brown them lightly very slowly over a low heat. Open the tin of peeled tomatoes, reserving the juice. Cut the tomatoes in half and remove the seeds. Mash the tomatoes roughly with a fork and pour them into the pan with their juice. Add the peas, salt and pepper. Cook over a low heat for 15 minutes.
4. Strain the spinach in a colander. Put the butter into a heavy pan. Add the spinach, cook for 10 minutes turning continuously, then add the fresh cream and mix well. Cook for a further 5 minutes over a high heat.
5. In a bowl, mix together the eggs, fresh cream and Gruyère cheese. Add salt, pepper and nutmeg. Divide the mixture into 3 to make 3 omelettes. Heat 5ml (1 tsp) of oil in a frying pan. Pour in the first omelette, lower the heat and allow to cook gently for 5 minutes. Turn the omelette by slipping it onto a plate and then returning it to the pan to cook on the other side for a further 5 minutes. Do this twice more with the rest of the mixture.
6. Set the oven at 205°C (400°F; gas mark 6). See if the tomato sauce has cooked and check the seasoning. Butter an ovenproof dish large enough to hold the omelettes tightly. Put in one omelette, cover it with a layer of spinach and half the tomato sauce. Do this once again, then top with the third omelette and finish with a layer of spinach. Put the dish in the oven for 10 minutes. Serve hot.

This 'cake' may be decorated with slices of Gruyère cheese.

Gâteau Vert
Green Cake

Serves 4. Preparation and cooking: 50 min

★★

○ **1kg (2¼ lb) spinach**
○ **200g (7 oz) soft white cheese: Ricotta or goat's milk cheese.**
○ **100g (4 oz) grated Parmesan or Gruyère cheese**
○ **1 garlic clove, finely chopped**
○ **15ml (1 tbls) chopped parsley**
○ **30ml (2 tbls) breadcrumbs**
○ **60g (3½ oz) butter**
○ **1 egg**
○ **salt and pepper**

1. Clean and wash the spinach with plenty of water. Do not drain. Put the leaves in a large saucepan, add salt and cover. Soften the leaves by cooking them in their own juice over a medium heat for 10 minutes.
2. When the spinach is ready, strain in a colander, pressing on the leaves. Chop the leaves roughly and put them in a bowl. Add the parsley, garlic, Parmesan and Ricotta. Season. Mix well, mashing the cheese with a fork. Add the egg. Mix again.
3. Set the oven at 220°C (425°F; gas mark 7).
4. Butter a mould or soufflé dish 22cm (10 inches) in diameter. Fill with half the mixture. Sprinkle the top with breadcrumbs and dot with knobs of butter. Put the dish in the oven for 20 minutes.
5. Serve very hot or very cold.

Épinards à la Tomate

Spinach with Tomatoes

Serves 4. Preparation: 30 min Cooking: 10 min

★★

- ○ **1kg (2¼ lb) spinach**
- ○ **800g (1¾ lb) ripe tomatoes**
- ○ **30ml (2 tbls) oil**
- ○ **60g (2½ oz) grated Gruyere cheese**
- ○ **50g (2 oz) butter**
- ○ **2.5ml (½ tsp) granulated sugar**
- ○ **2.5ml (½ tsp) marjoram**
- ○ **salt and pepper**

1. Cut the stalks off the spinach, wash the leaves but do not drain. Put the leaves in a large saucepan, and cook in their own juice for 5 minutes over a high heat, covered, then strain in a colander, pressing to eliminate all the water. Plunge the tomatoes into boiling water for 30 seconds then drain them and put under cold running water. Peel, cut them in half, press to remove the seeds and chop roughly.
2. Heat the oil in a large frying pan and put in the tomatoes. Add the sugar, salt, pepper and marjoram. Cook for 5 minutes over a high heat, turning continuously, then remove from the heat.
3. Set the oven at 230°C (450°F; gas mark 8). Butter a large gratin dish with 20g (1 oz) butter. Put in the spinach, pour over the tomato sauce, sprinkle with cheese and dot with the rest of the butter. Put the dish in the oven for 10 minutes. Serve very hot from the dish.

Épinards au Gratin

Spinach Gratin

Serves 4. Preparation and cooking: 40 min

★★

- ○ **1kg (2¼ lb) spinach**
- ○ **250ml (9 fl oz) milk**
- ○ **15ml (1 tbls) cornflour**
- ○ **1 egg yolk**
- ○ **100g (4 oz) grated Gruyère cheese**
- ○ **40g (1¾ oz) butter**
- ○ **100ml (3½ fl oz) cold water**
- ○ **salt and pepper**
- ○ **pinch nutmeg**

1. Cut the stalks off the spinach and wash the leaves, then blanch them for 3 minutes in salted boiling water; strain in a colander, pressing on the leaves to eliminate all the water.
2. In a bowl, mix the egg yolk with 15ml (1 tbls) of milk. Mix the cornflour with 100ml (3½ fl oz) cold water.
3. Pour the rest of the milk into a saucepan. Add salt, pepper and nutmeg. Bring to the boil and add the diluted starch. Mix well and allow to boil for 2 minutes, turning continuously. Then remove from the heat, leave to cool and blend in the egg yolk and 70g (3 oz) of grated cheese. Mix again. Check the seasoning.
4. Set the oven at 220°C (425°F; gas mark 7). Grease a gratin dish with 20g (1 oz) butter. Arrange the spinach on it and cover with sauce. Sprinkle with the remaining cheese and dot with knobs of butter.
5. Put the dish in the oven for 15 minutes and serve immediately.

Legumes (pulses) are beans, lentils and peas picked when ripe, then dried. The best legumes are those which are less than one year old. If they are older than this they will have deteriorated and become indigestible. They should always be soaked for several hours – at most overnight – before cooking to replace the water lost in the drying process. If you soak them for too long they may ferment and become completely uneatable. Unlike fresh vegetables, dried beans and pulses should be put into cold water to cook, which should cover them well as they will continue to swell during cooking. Once they have come to the boil, the heat should be turned very low and they should be left to simmer slowly. When the simmering begins, skim the surface, add a bouquet garni, an onion spiked with cloves, a carrot, and one or more cloves of garlic. Cover the pan and cook until tender. Do not allow to boil, otherwise they will burst. Add salt after 30 minutes of cooking. If the liquid dries up, add more water but it must be boiling, since cold water will arrest the cooking and harden the vegetables.

If they are prepared carefully like this, dried beans and pulses can be used as the basis for more elaborate recipes, or they can be served plain with a little butter or puréed. They can be prepared as a salad, served cold or lukewarm.

Choux de Bruxelles au Jambon (p40)▶

Endives Sautées à la Crème

Serves 4. Preparation and cooking: 50 min

Chicory Sautéed with Cream

★★

- 1kg (2¼ lb) large heads chicory
- 3 thin rashers smoked bacon
- 30g (1⅛ oz) butter
- 100ml (3½ fl oz) dry white wine
- 100ml (3½ fl oz) water
- 200g (7 oz) fresh cream
- 15ml (1 tbls) chopped parsley
- salt and pepper

1. Remove the outer leaves of the chicory, and wash carefully. Hollow out the bitter core with a small pointed knife. Blanch the heads for 10 minutes in salted boiling water.
2. Meanwhile, cut the bacon into sticks 1cm (½ inch) wide. Melt the butter in a heavy pan, add the bacon and lightly brown over a low heat to prevent the butter burning.
3. When the chicory is blanched, strain, and add to the pan. Lightly brown them on all sides by turning continuously. Add the water and the wine. Add salt, pepper and cook uncovered for 20 minutes over a low heat; turn the chicory two or three times during the cooking.
4. At the end of this time, add the fresh cream and reduce it for 5 minutes over a high heat. Sprinkle with chopped parsley and serve hot.

Endives au Lait

Serves 4. Preparation and cooking: 35 min

Chicory with Milk

★★

- 4 good heads chicory
- 1 large chopped onion
- 250ml (9 fl oz) milk
- 50g (2 oz) grated Parmesan or Gruyère cheese
- 30ml (2 tbls) oil
- salt and pepper
- pinch nutmeg

1. Remove the outer leaves of the chicory, and wash carefully. Hollow out the bitter core with a small pointed knife. Blanch the heads for 5 minutes in salted boiling water.
2. Pour the oil into a heavy pan, and add the well-chopped onion. Brown lightly over a low heat.
3. Carefully strain the chicory and add to the pan on top of the layer of onion. Add salt, pour in the milk and cook uncovered for 20 minutes over a low heat.
4. Mix the grated cheese with the pepper and nutmeg and sprinkle over the chicory. Allow the cheese to melt and serve immediately.

Salade d'Endives aux Noix

Serves 4. Preparation: 15 min

Chicory and Walnut Salad

★

- 4 medium-sized heads chicory
- 50g (2 oz) shelled walnuts
- 45ml (3 tbls) oil
- 30ml (2 tbls) vinegar
- 2.5ml (½ tsp) sugar
- salt and pepper

1. Roughly chop the walnuts. Remove the outer leaves of chicory. Hollow out the bitter core with a small pointed knife. Wash the heads quickly with cold water, dry them in a cloth and cut them into rounds 1cm (½ inch) thick.
2. Prepare the dressing. In a bowl mix the vinegar, sugar, salt and pepper with a fork. Add the oil, mixing all the time.
3. Put the chicory into a salad bowl, add the walnuts and pour over the dressing. Mix everything very well and serve immediately.

In Italy they do not blanch spinach by boiling in an uncovered saucepan, in a large quantity of salted water. Instead, having washed the spinach, they put it into a large saucepan without draining it. Salt is added, and the pan is covered and placed over a high heat. After 5 minutes, the spinach is fané *(limp) and ready to be used as you want.*

Fèves à la Paysanne
Broad Beans Peasant-Style

Serves 4. Preparation: 20 min Cooking: 1 hr

★★

○ **1.5kg (3¼ lb) broad beans**
○ **100g (4 oz) smoked bacon**
○ **1 large onion**
○ **500g (1 lb) small new potatoes**
○ **4 small smoked sausages**
○ **30g (1 oz) butter**
○ **1 chicken stock cube**
○ **250ml (9 fl oz) hot water**
○ **salt and pepper**

1. Shell the beans and slip off the tough skins. Peel and chop the onion. Cut the bacon into sticks.
2. Melt the butter in a pan and lightly brown the onion and the bacon, then add the beans. Dissolve the stock cube in hot water. Pour the stock into the pan and simmer for 30 minutes over a low heat.
3. Meanwhile, scrape the potatoes, wash them, and leave to soak in cold water. After the beans have cooked for 30 minutes, strain the potatoes and put them into the pan. Add salt and pepper, and cook for a further 20 minutes.
4. At the end of this time slice the sausages into rounds across and add to the pan. Cook for another 10 minutes.
5. When the cooking is finished, very little stock should be left in the pan. If too much remains, remove the lid and reduce the liquid by rapid boiling. Serve this dish very hot.

Fèves à la Romaine
Broad Beans Roman-Style

Serves 4. Preparation: 15 min Cooking: 50 min approx

★★

○ **1.5kg (3¼ lb) fresh broad beans**
○ **100g (4 oz) raw ham or mild-cured bacon**
○ **2 lettuce hearts**
○ **1 large onion**
○ **1 chicken stock cube**
○ **250ml (9 fl oz) water**
○ **50g (2 oz) butter**
○ **salt and pepper**

1. Shell the beans and slip off their tough skins. Peel and chop the onion. Cut the ham (or bacon) into fine strips. Separate the lettuce leaves. Wash them and cut into strips 1cm (½ inch) wide.
2. Melt the butter in a heavy pan and lightly brown the onion and the ham. Add the beans. Add very little salt, as the stock will contain salt. Add pepper. Cook for 10 minutes over a low heat, turning the beans often, then add the lettuce. Mix well.
3. Dissolve the stock cube in hot water and pour into the pan. Cover. Leave to simmer for about 30 minutes, until the beans are tender. Serve very hot.

Toast may be served with this dish.

Fèves aux Poivrons
Broad Beans with Peppers

Serves 4. Preparation: 10 min Cooking: 55 min

★

○ **1.5kg (3¼ lb) fresh broad beans**
○ **1 red pepper**
○ **1 large onion**
○ **30g (1¼ oz) butter**
○ **100ml (3½ fl oz) water**
○ **2 pinches sugar**
○ **salt and pepper**

1. Shell the beans and slip off their tough skins. Simmer the beans gently for 30 minutes in boiling, salted water.
2. Meanwhile, wash the peppers, cut them in half lengthways and take out the seeds. Cut them into thin strips. Peel and chop the onion finely.
3. Put the butter into a pan and lightly brown the onions and the peppers over a low heat.
4. Strain the beans and put them into the pan. Add the water and the sugar. Add salt and pepper. Simmer uncovered over a low heat for 15 minutes, adding a little water if necessary. Serve very hot.

Fenouils à la Mayonnaise

Serves 6. Preparation and cooking: 35 min

Fennel with Mayonnaise

★★

○ **6 medium-sized heads fennel**
○ **45ml (3 tbls) pickles**
○ **15ml (1 tbls) chopped parsley**

For the mayonnaise:
○ **1 egg yolk**
○ **5ml (1 tsp) mustard**
○ **100ml (3½ fl oz) oil**
○ **30ml (2 tbls) fresh cream**
○ **salt**

1. Remove the tough outer leaves of the fennel and cut off the stalks. Wash the rest and cook in salted boiling water for about 20 minutes until they are tender.
2. Prepare the mayonnaise. In a bowl put the egg yolk and the mustard. Beat quickly with a whisk. Put in the oil drop by drop, beating vigorously all the time. Add salt. When the mayonnaise is ready, fold in the fresh cream.
3. Strain the fennel and leave to cool. Cut each head into 4, but do not cut right through. Arrange them on a serving dish, sprinkle the dish with pickles and then cover all with cream mayonnaise. Sprinkle with parsley and serve cold.

Pickles are vegetables that have been grated, cubed or sliced and preserved in vinegar. They are salty, sweet and spicy all at the same time.

Fenouils aux Olives Noires

Serves 4. Preparation and cooking: 30 min

Fennel with Black Olives

★

○ **3 large heads fennel**
○ **2 anchovy fillets, canned**
○ **1 hard-boiled egg**
○ **30ml (2 tbls) vinegar**
○ **75ml (5 tbls) oil**
○ **50g (2 oz) pitted black olives**
○ **salt and pepper**

1. Remove the tough outer leaves of the fennel and cut off the stalks. Cut the heads into 4, wash and drain. Cook in salted boiling water for about 20 minutes until they are tender.
2. Meanwhile, mash the egg yolk with a fork in a bowl. Chop the anchovies, add them to the egg, and mix in the vinegar. Add a little salt and pepper. Blend in the oil little by little, beating with a fork.
3. When the fennel is cooked, strain and leave to cool. Arrange the fennel on a serving dish. Coat with the sauce. Chop the egg white and the olives, and sprinkle the fennel with this mixture. Serve.

Salade de Fenouils au Roquefort

Serves 4. Preparation: 15 min

Fennel Salad with Roquefort Cheese

★

○ **2 large heads fennel**

For the sauce:
○ **50g (2 oz) Roquefort cheese**
○ **50g (2 oz) fresh cream**
○ **15ml (1 tbls) vinegar**
○ **30ml (2 tbls) oil**
○ **15ml (1 tbls) chopped walnuts**
○ **salt and pepper**

1. Cut off the stalks of the fennel. Remove the tough outer leaves. Cut the heads into 4 and wash them. Chop finely and put into a salad bowl.
2. In a bowl, crumble the Roquefort with a fork. Add the vinegar and the fresh cream, the oil and walnuts. Add very little salt, and some pepper. Mix well.
3. Pour this sauce over the fennel. Mix again.

Serve immediately, adding if desired chopped herbs or chives.

Do not hesitate to scrunch raw young spinach leaves! As a salad they can be eaten with a vinaigrette made with oil or cream, with walnuts or grated nuts added, or a crushed garlic clove or a shallot, or slices of Roquefort. It is delicious!

Haricots Verts au Persil

Serves 4. Preparation: 10 min Cooking: 35 min approx

French Beans with Parsley

★

○ **750g (1 lb 10 oz) French beans**
○ **2 large onions cut into thin rounds**
○ **45ml (3 tbls) chopped parsley**
○ **2.5ml (½ tsp) thyme flowers**
○ **2.5ml (½ tsp) savory**
○ **juice of 1 lemon**
○ **60ml (4 tbls) oil**
○ **½ litre (18 fl oz; 1 pint) hot water**
○ **salt and pepper**

1. Top and tail, wash and drain the beans. Cook them in salted, boiling water for 10 minutes, then strain.
2. Heat the oil in a heavy pan and lightly brown the onion rounds. Put these on one side.
3. Put a layer of beans into the pan, then a layer of onions, sprinkle with parsley, thyme and savory. Continue in this fashion until the ingredients are used up. Sprinkle with lemon juice. Add salt and pepper and pour in the hot water. Cover the pan and cook for 15 minutes over a low heat, then remove the cover, raise the heat, and allow the liquid to reduce. Leave to cool before serving.

Purée de Haricots Verts

Serves 4. Preparation and cooking: 1 hr 50 min

Purée of French Beans

★★

○ **1kg (2¼ lb) large French beans**
○ **125g (5 oz) fresh cream**
○ **salt and pepper**

1. Top and tail, and wash the French beans. Cook in salted, boiling water for 25 minutes until they are tender.
2. When the beans are cooked strain them. Pass them through a sieve or blender to purée. Leave the purée to drain through a muslin cloth for at least 1 hour.
3. At the end of this time, put the cream in a saucepan and reduce it by half over a high heat. Then lower the flame and add the bean purée. Add salt and pepper. Mix well with a wooden spoon.
4. Serve the purée as soon as it is hot.

This purée, possibly served with croûtons browned in butter, goes well with all kinds of meat and also with grilled or poached fish.

Haricots Blancs à l'Étouffée

Serves 4. Preparation: 15 min Cooking: 1 hr 10 min

White Bean Stew

★★

○ **1kg (2¼ lb) white haricot beans (in pods)**
○ **1 small onion**
○ **1 leek**
○ **50g (2 oz) lean mild-cured bacon**
○ **1 garlic clove**
○ **15ml (1 tbls) chopped parsley**
○ **1 bay leaf**
○ **30ml (2 tbls) tomato concentrate**
○ **30g (1¼ oz) butter**
○ **30ml (2 tbls) oil**
○ **salt and pepper**

1. Shell the beans, wash and drain them. Peel and chop the onion. Clean the leek and cut into thin rounds 2mm (⅛ inch) thick. Peel and chop the garlic finely. Cut the bacon into thin sticks.
2. Heat the oil in a heavy pan, add the butter, onion, leek, bacon, garlic and parsley. Lightly brown everything, then add the beans and the bay leaf. Cover with cold water. Bring to the boil. Add salt and pepper. Cover the pan and simmer for 45 minutes over a low heat.
3. At the end of this time, dilute the tomato concentrate in 15ml (1 tbls) of water and pour it into the pan. Mix, leave to simmer for a further 15 minutes.

Serve hot to accompany braised or roast meat: duck, pork, or lamb.

Haricots à la Lombarde

Serves 4. Preparation and cooking: 1 hr 45 min

Haricot Beans with Vegetables

★★

○ **1kg (2¼ lb) haricot beans (in pods)**
○ **3 sage leaves**
○ **1 garlic clove, chopped small**
○ **1 small onion**
○ **15ml (1 tbls) chopped parsley**
○ **1 stick celery**
○ **1 carrot**
○ **100ml (3½ fl oz) oil**
○ **15ml (1 tbls) tomato concentrate**
○ **200ml (7 fl oz) hot water**
○ **1 stock cube**
○ **salt and pepper**

Optional:
○ **10 cabbage leaves (cooked)**

1. Shell and wash the beans.
2. Put the beans into a saucepan and cover with cold water. Add the garlic and sage. Bring to the boil and add salt, then cover and cook for about 1 hour 15 minutes over a low heat until the beans are soft. Watch the cooking and add a little water if necessary, stirring now and then to avoid any beans sticking to the bottom of the pan.
3. 30 minutes before the beans are cooked, peel the onion and string the celery. Wash and chop finely. Peel the carrot, wash and chop as fine as possible. Dissolve the stock cube in hot water.
4. Heat some oil in a heavy pan and lightly brown the chopped vegetables. Add salt and pepper, then the parsley, tomato concentrate and stock. Stir together well.
5. Strain the beans and add them to the pan. Stir well. Cover and cook for about 10 minutes. 5 minutes before the end of cooking the cooked cabbage leaves may be added.

Serve hot, accompanied if wished by croûtons fried in butter until golden.

Salade Tiède de Haricots Blancs

Serves 4. Preparation and cooking: 1 hr 15 min

White Bean Salad, served warm

★

○ **1.5kg (3¼ lb) white haricot beans (in pods)**
○ **1 celery heart**
○ **1 onion**
○ **2 carrots**
○ **1 sprig thyme**
○ **1 bay leaf**
○ **1 clove**
○ **4 spring onions**
○ **100ml (3½ fl oz) oil**
○ **45ml (3 tbls) vinegar**
○ **5ml (1 tsp) strong mustard**
○ **15ml (1 tbls) chopped parsley**
○ **salt and pepper**

1. Shell the beans and wash them. Put in a large saucepan and cover with plenty of cold water. Bring to the boil over a medium heat.
2. Peel and wash the carrots. Peel the onion and spike it with the clove. Clean the celery heart. Add these vegetables to the saucepan, with the sprig of thyme and the bay leaf.
3. When the water begins to boil, add salt and lower the heat, continue cooking by simmering slowly without a lid for about 45 minutes until the beans are tender.
4. When the beans are cooked, strain them in a sieve. Remove the thyme, bay leaf and onion. Slice the carrots and celery across, and put them back with the beans.
5. Put the mustard, vinegar, salt and pepper in a bowl, and add the oil while beating with a fork to emulsify the sauce. Peel the spring onions, chop them and add them to the vinaigrette.
6. Put the beans into a salad bowl. Sprinkle with the vinaigrette, mix well, sprinkle with chopped parsley and serve immediately.

To make a separate course of this delicious salad add some flaked canned tuna fish or some small bacon cubes browned in a frying pan.

The cooking times indicated in each recipe should not be followed absolutely; test to see if the vegetables are tender and alter accordingly. Cooking vegetables requires the same amount of care as cooking meat, game or fish. Generally speaking, vegetables are spoiled by being overcooked. Did you know that spinach needs only 4 minutes cooking in water and that fresh-picked French beans, too, need no longer than that?

Haricots Frais au Lard

Serves 4. Preparation and cooking: 1 hr 50 min approx

Fresh Haricot Beans with Bacon

★★

○ **1kg (2¼ lb) haricot beans (in pods)**
○ **100g (4 oz) smoked bacon**
○ **2 medium-sized onions**
○ **20g (¾ oz) butter**
○ **30ml (2 tbls) oil**
○ **1 stock cube**
○ **salt and pepper**

1. Shell and wash the haricot beans and put them into a large saucepan, covering with plenty of cold water. Add salt. Cook covered over a low heat for about 1 hour until tender.
2. At the end of this time, peel the onions and cut them into thick circles. Cut the bacon into strips 1cm (½ inch) wide.
3. Heat the oil in a heavy pan, add the butter, then the onions and bacon. Lightly brown over a low heat.
4. Strain the haricot beans, keeping back 250ml (9 fl oz) of the cooking water. Pour this over the stock cube.
5. Put the beans into the dish; mix in the bacon strips and the onions with a wooden spoon, then add the stock. Add salt and pepper, and mix.
6. Cook uncovered over a medium heat for about 20 minutes until the stock has completely evaporated. Serve very hot.

Haricot Verts au Yaourt

Serves 4. Preparation: 10 min Cooking: 30 min

French Beans with Yogurt

★★

○ **750g (1 lb 10 oz) French beans**
○ **1 large onion**
○ **150g (6 oz) cooked ham**
○ **2 eggs**
○ **1 carton yogurt**
○ **50g (2 oz) grated Gruyère cheese**
○ **1 garlic clove**
○ **15ml (1 tbls) chopped parsley**
○ **30ml (2 tbls) oil**
○ **20g (¾ oz) butter**
○ **5ml (1 tsp) mild paprika**
○ **salt and pepper**

1. Top and tail, wash and drain the French beans. Cook the beans in salted, boiling water for 10 minutes; they should remain slightly crunchy. Strain.
2. Meanwhile, peel the garlic and onion and chop them very small. Cut the ham into thin slices.
3. Heat some oil in a frying pan and lightly brown the garlic, onion and ham. Add the French beans and cook for 5 minutes, stirring well, then sprinkle with chopped parsley.
4. Set the oven at 220°C (425°F; gas mark 7).
5. Butter a gratin dish and put the beans in it.
6. Beat the eggs well in a bowl, and add the yogurt, half the cheese, and the paprika. Season. Pour this mixture onto the beans. Sprinkle with the remaining cheese.
7. Put the dish in the oven for 15 minutes and serve immediately.

Green vegetables cooked in boiling water – French beans, peas, spinach, asparagus – should be cooked only for a short time so that they remain crunchy. To do this, plunge them into a large amount of salted boiling water – 10g-20g (½ oz-¾ oz) sea salt per litre (1¾ pints) water – and boil hard without a lid. Watch the cooking carefully to make sure the vegetables are not overcooked but remain firm. Strain them straight away, season, and serve immediately. Green vegetables prepared in this way, served with a knob of butter and chopped herbs and with no other seasoning, make a delicious dish.

If the vegetables are not to be served immediately, strain them just the same, and plunge them into a basin of cold – even iced – water, then strain again. Before serving, plunge the vegetables a second time into boiling water to reheat them without actually re-cooking them. Treated this way, the vegetables will retain their colour and their crunchiness.

Haricots Verts aux Quatre Fromages

French Beans with 4 Kinds of Cheese

Serves 6.
Preparation and cooking: 50 min
★★

○ **1kg (2¼ lb) thin French beans**
○ **100g (4 oz) butter**
○ **100g (4 oz) Gruyère cheese**
○ **100g (4 oz) tomme de Savoie (Savoy cheese)**
○ **50g (2 oz) grated Parmesan cheese**
○ **100g (4 oz) Gouda cheese**
○ **1 egg**
○ **15ml (1 tbls) flour**
○ **250ml (9 fl oz) milk**
○ **salt and pepper**
○ **pinch nutmeg**

1. Top and tail the French beans, wash them and blanch for 10 minutes in salted boiling water. Strain.
2. Meanwhile, cut the cheeses into thin strips.
3. Melt 50g (2 oz) butter in a frying pan and cook the beans for 5 minutes. Leave them to cool, then sprinkle with Parmesan and add the sliced cheese.
4. Prepare the béchamel sauce: melt 30g (1¼ oz) butter in a pan, add the flour, turning constantly, then blend in the milk very gradually. Cook for 5 minutes then remove from the heat and add the egg, beating all the time with a fork. Add salt and pepper and nutmeg. Pour the béchamel over the beans.
5. Set the oven at 230°C (450°F; gas mark 8).
6. Grease a gratin dish with the remaining butter. Pour in the beans and put the dish into the oven for 10 minutes to allow the cheese to melt. Then serve.

Haricots Verts aux Anchois

French Beans with Anchovies

Serves 4. Preparation: 10 min Cooking: 30 min
★

○ **750g (1 lb 10 oz) French beans**
○ **1 garlic clove**
○ **1 small onion**
○ **6 anchovy fillets**
○ **10 sprigs parsley**
○ **60ml (4 tbls) oil**
○ **salt**
○ **8 basil leaves (optional)**

1. Top and tail, wash and drain the French beans. Cook for about 10 minutes in salted, boiling water: they should remain slightly crisp.
2. Peel the garlic clove and the onion and chop finely. Wash the basil and the parsley, wipe them and chop.
3. When the beans are cooked, strain them.
4. Heat some oil in a pan, add the onion and the garlic and brown them lightly over a low heat. Add the anchovies, crushing them with a spatula, then add the beans. Mix together well and cook for 10 minutes over a low heat.
5. Sprinkle with parsley and chopped basil and cook for a further 5 minutes. Serve immediately.

Haricots Beurre à la Toscane

Butter Beans with Tomato and Bacon

Serves 4. Preparation: 15 min Cooking: 25 min
★

○ **750g (1 lb 10 oz) fresh butter beans**
○ **500g (1 lb) ripe tomatoes**
○ **50g (2 oz) smoked bacon**
○ **2 garlic cloves**
○ **60ml (4 tbls) oil**
○ **100ml (3½ fl oz) cold water**
○ **pinch cayenne pepper**
○ **salt and pepper**
○ **4 fresh basil leaves (optional)**

1. Clean the beans, wash and drain them. Plunge the tomatoes in boiling water for 30 seconds, strain and hold them under cold running water. Peel them, cut in half, removing all the seeds, mash roughly with a fork. Peel and chop the garlic. Cut the bacon into thin sticks.
2. Put the butter beans in a heavy pan with the tomatoes, bacon, cayenne pepper and the garlic. Add the oil and cold water, and season. Cover the pan and cook over a low heat for about 25 minutes until the beans are tender.
3. Before serving, chop the basil leaves and sprinkle over the dish. Serve.

Lentilles à la Paysanne
Lentils Peasant-Style

Serves 4. Preparation: 20 min Cooking: 1 hr 50 min

★★

- ○ **400g (14 oz) green lentils**
- ○ **200g (7 oz) smoked bacon**
- ○ **1 large onion**
- ○ **2 carrots**
- ○ **2 turnips**
- ○ **1 stick celery**
- ○ **1 bouquet garni consisting of:**
  10 sprigs parsley, 1 bay leaf,
  1 sprig thyme
- ○ **1 peeled garlic clove**
- ○ **40g (1¾ oz) butter**
- ○ **15ml (1 tbls) flour**
- ○ **salt and pepper**

1. Sort and wash the lentils. Put them in a large saucepan and cover with cold water. Bring to the boil over a low heat. Boil for 3 minutes then strain.
2. Peel and chop the onion well. Peel the carrots and the turnips, wash them and dice them as small as possible.
3. Melt the butter in a large pan and lightly brown the vegetables, then sprinkle with flour. Mix together with a wooden spoon and pour on 1 litre (1¾ pints) of water. Bring to the boil, then add the lentils, bacon and garlic.
4. Tie together the herbs for the bouquet garni. Clean the celery. Add both to the pan. Season. Pour in 2 litres (3½ pints) of water: this should cover the lentils well to allow them to swell up during cooking. Cover the pan and cook over a low heat for about 1 hour 30 minutes until the lentils are soft. Remove the bouquet garni and serve.

This dish can be enriched by adding braised or grilled pork sausages.

Lentilles au Lard
Lentils with Bacon

Serves 4. Preparation: 20 min Cooking: 1 hr 30 min

★

- ○ **400g (14 oz) green lentils**
- ○ **150g (6 oz) mild-cured bacon**
- ○ **1 medium-sized onion**
- ○ **2 cloves**
- ○ **1 bouquet garni consisting of:**
  10 sprigs parsley, 1 bay leaf,
  1 sprig thyme
- ○ **1 peeled garlic clove**
- ○ **salt and pepper**

1. Sort the lentils and wash them. Strain and put in a pan, cover well with cold water.
2. Peel the onion and spike it with the cloves. Tie up the bouquet garni. Put both into the pan and add the garlic. Bring to the boil over a very low heat. This will take about 45 minutes.
3. Cut the bacon into sticks about 1cm (½ inch) wide. As soon as the lentils begin to boil, add the bacon, salt, and pepper. Cover the pan and continue cooking over a low heat for about 45 minutes until the lentils are tender and almost all the liquid has evaporated.
4. Before serving, remove the onion and the bouquet garni.

Hot lentils make an excellent accompaniment to roast pork, grilled sausages or boiled salt pork. Hot or cold, seasoned with a vinaigrette dressing and chopped onions, they make a delicious salad.

Broccoli: the name is Italian in origin and there are at least four different types in France. Two at least are quite common in Great Britain: purple broccoli and calabrese or green broccoli. This has dark green leaves arranged around tight heads or tiny buds on a central stem. Its taste, although sweeter, is like that of green cabbage. It is delicious in a salad, whether hot, warm or cold, seasoned with oil and vinegar or lemon. Purple broccoli is half-leaf, half-flower: smooth leaves, slightly blue-ish in colour, grow round a central stem surrounding one or more heads of the same colour, made up of hundreds of small buds which if allowed to grow would later open into beautiful yellow flowers.

Purée de Navets
Purée of Turnip

Serves 4. Preparation and cooking: 50 min

○ **1kg (2¼ lb) turnips**
○ **300g (11 oz) potatoes**
○ **150g (6 oz) fresh double cream**
○ **salt and pepper**

1. Peel the turnips, wash them and cut into 4. Peel the potatoes, wash them and dice. Cook the turnips and potatoes in salted, boiling water for about 30 minutes until they are very tender.
2. When the vegetables are cooked, strain them and put them through a fine sieve or blender.
3. Put the purée and the cream into a saucepan and heat through, stirring with a wooden spoon to prevent the bottom from scorching. Add salt and pepper. Allow the purée to reduce for several minutes if it is too liquid, and serve immediately or keep hot until serving.

This purée is delicious with pork, duck and goose.

Navets Glacés
Glazed Turnips

Serves 4. Preparation: 10 min Cooking: 45 min

○ **1kg (2¼ lb) small turnips**
○ **100g (4 oz) butter**
○ **15ml (1 tbls) granulated sugar**
○ **150ml (5 fl oz) hot water**
○ **salt**

1. Peel the turnips and trim them to a walnut shape. Wash, drain and wipe them.
2. Melt the butter in a saucepan which is large enough to hold the turnips without any overlapping and brown them lightly. Add salt, then sprinkle with sugar. Leave them to caramelize; then pour in hot water and leave to cook for 35 minutes over a low heat, shaking the saucepan to ensure that the turnips cook uniformly without turning them, since they are very fragile.
3. At the end of the cooking time, there should be no liquid left in the saucepan apart from a honey-like juice.

Serve these turnips very hot to accompany braised or roast pork, goose or duck.

Navets Farcis
Stuffed Turnips

Serves 4. Preparation: 30 min Cooking: 1 hr 30 min

★★★

○ **8 large round turnips**
○ **100g (4 oz) cooked ham**
○ **100g (4 oz) veal**
○ **100g (4 oz) sausagemeat**
○ **30ml (2 tbls) chopped parsley**
○ **50g (2 oz) grated Gruyère cheese**
○ **1 egg**
○ **50g (2 oz) butter**
○ **15ml (1 tbls) port**
○ **1 stock cube**
○ **250ml (9 fl oz) hot water**
○ **salt and pepper**

1. Peel and wash the turnips. Cut across the top 1cm (½ inch) deep to make a cap. Hollow out the centre with a small pointed knife without breaking the turnips.
2. Chop the ham and the veal, mash the sausagemeat. Mix everything together in a bowl, add the Gruyère cheese, parsley and port. Season. Add the egg. Mix again.
3. Stuff the turnips and put their 'caps' back on.
4. Set the oven at 195°C (375°F; gas mark 5). Prepare the stock by dissolving the cube in hot water.
5. Butter a gratin dish, arrange the turnips on it and pour over half the stock. Cook for 1 hour 30 minutes adding a little stock to the dish as the liquid reduces.

The ham and sausagemeat may be replaced by fresh pork and chicken.

Fenouils aux Olives Noires (p46) ▶

Tourte aux Oignons

Egg and Onion Pie

Serves 4. Preparation and cooking: 1 hr 15 min

★★★

○ **600g (1 lb 5 oz) onions**
○ **100g (4 oz) smoked bacon**
○ **2 whole eggs**
○ **2 egg yolks**
○ **20g (1 oz) butter**
○ **30ml (2 tbls) oil**
○ **salt and pepper**
○ **pinch nutmeg**

For the shortcrust pastry:
○ **250g (9 oz) flour**
○ **180g (7¼ oz) soft butter**
○ **60ml (4 tbls) water**
○ **salt**

For the glaze:
○ **1 egg yolk**
○ **15ml (1 tbls) water**

1. Peel the onions and chop well. Dice the bacon as small as possible.
2. Put the oil in a frying pan and cook the onions and the bacon over a very low heat until the onions are transparent but not brown.
3. Prepare the shortcrust pastry. Make a well in the centre of the flour and add the salt, water and butter. Progressively work the butter into the flour until it is thoroughly incorporated. Knead the pastry until it comes away from the fingers to make one large ball.
4. Set the oven at 220°C (425°F; gas mark 7). Grease a pie dish 30cm (10 inches) in diameter.
5. Divide the pastry into two. Roll out one half to cover the base and sides of the pie dish.
6. Beat two eggs, plus the yolks from two more, in a bowl and add the onions and bacon. Season with salt, pepper and nutmeg. Pour the mixture into the pastry.
7. Roll out the other half of the pastry to make a lid. Trim off the extra pastry; press the edges together well and scallop. Make a glaze by mixing the egg yolk with a little water and brush the top of the pastry with it.
8. Place the pie in the oven and cook for about 40 minutes.
9. This pie can be eaten hot, warm or cold. Serve it at the start of the meal, or as a main course with a salad in season.

Soufflé d'Oignons aux Asperges

Onion and Asparagus Soufflé

Serves 4. Preparation and cooking: 1 hr

★★★

○ **500g (1 lb 2 oz) onions**
○ **500g (1 lb 2 oz) asparagus**
○ **3 eggs, separated**
○ **100ml (3½ fl oz) oil**
○ **50g (2 oz) grated Parmesan or Gruyère cheese**
○ **20g (¾ oz) butter**
○ **15ml (1 tbls) flour**
○ **salt and pepper**
○ **pinch nutmeg**

1. Peel the onions and chop them well. Scrape or peel the asparagus and cut into segments 2cm (¾ inch) long, using the top two-third of the stalk only.
2. Cook the asparagus gently in boiling salted water for 20 minutes.
3. Meanwhile, add the oil to a frying pan and sauté the onions over a low heat, turning constantly. When they are golden, leave them to cool, then put them through a sieve or blender. Add the egg yolks and cheese to this purée and season with salt, pepper and nutmeg.
4. Set the oven at 205°C (400°F; gas mark 6).
5. Strain the asparagus in a colander. Dip each stalk in flour before adding it to the onion purée.
6. Fold the stiffly-whipped egg whites carefully into the mixture.
7. Butter a soufflé dish double the volume of the mixture. Pour in the mixture and cook in the oven for 25 minutes.
8. Serve immediately.

If a sauce or mixture is too thick you should thin it by diluting it with an appropriate liquid. For instance, potato purée is diluted with milk, which you should pour in gradually, stirring all the time to make sure no lumps form until you achieve the consistency you want.

Petits Oignons Glacés

Serves 4. Preparation: 10 min Cooking: 1 hr 10 min

Glazed White Onions

★

○ **1kg (2¼ lb) small white onions**
○ **60g (2½ oz) butter**
○ **45ml (3 tbls) vinegar**
○ **15ml (1 tbls) sugar**
○ **200ml (7 fl oz) water**
○ **salt**

1. Peel the onions and leave them whole. Heat the oil in a frying pan, add the butter and brown the onions lightly. Add salt and sprinkle with sugar. When the onions have caramelized add the vinegar and water.
2. Cover the pan and cook for 1 hour over a low heat, turning the onions now and then. At the end of this time reduce any liquid left in the pan by cooking uncovered over a high heat.

These flavoursome onions should be served as an accompaniment to roast meat, especially pork.

Feuilleté aux Oignons

Serves 4. Preparation and cooking: 1 hr

Flaky Onion Tart

★ ★

○ **1.5kg (3¼ lb) small white onions (in a bunch)**
○ **60ml (4 tbls) oil**
○ **20g (¾ oz) butter**
○ **500g (18 fl oz) frozen flaky pastry**
○ **salt and pepper**

1. Thaw the pastry according to the instructions.
2. Trim and peel the onions, keeping at least 3cm (1 inch) of the green part; slice them very thin. Heat the oil in a frying pan and brown the onions. Season, cover the pan and continue cooking over a very low heat for 15 minutes.
3. Set the oven at 230°C (450°F; gas mark 8). Grease a rectangular oven tray.
4. Roll out the pastry so it is 0.5cm (1/6 inch) thick and place it on the oven tray, trimming the edges. Spread the pastry with the onions.
5. Put the tray in the oven for 20 minutes. Serve hot or warm.

Oignons Nouveaux Confits

Serves 6. Preparation: 15 min Cooking: 1 hr approx

Pickled Onions

★

○ **1kg (2¼ lb) small pickling onions (about 50 onions)**
○ **100ml (3½ fl oz) malt vinegar**
○ **30ml (2 tbls) sultanas**
○ **30ml (2 tbls) sugar**
○ **30ml (2 tbls) oil**
○ **30ml (2 tbls) tomato concentrate**
○ **2 cloves**
○ **1 bay leaf**
○ **2ml (½ tsp) salt**

1. Peel the onions and cut off the tails.
2. Put the onions in a large pan and add the sultanas, vinegar, tomato concentrate, sugar, cloves, bay leaf and salt. Cover amply with cold water. Bring to the boil, stirring with a wooden spoon, then lower the heat and cook very gently for about 1 hour, without a lid. At the end of this time nearly all the liquid should have evaporated, leaving only a thick syrup to coat the onions.
3. Allow the onions to cool and place in the refrigerator. They can be eaten several hours later, the following day, or several days later.

These tangy onions may be served with all cold meats, or to start a meal on slices of toasted bread.

You 'sweat' meat or vegetables by cooking them in a covered pan without any fat: they 'sweat' out all their own liquid. Shallots and onions are treated in this way, which is the opposite of allowing them to brown, without a lid, in butter, oil or some other fat.

Oignons Farcis au Saumon

Serves 4. Preparation: 30 min Cooking: 50 min

Onions Stuffed with Salmon

★ ★ ★

- ○ **8 large onions**
- ○ **40g (1¾ oz) smoked salmon**
- ○ **250g (9 oz) cooked white chicken**
- ○ **1 egg**
- ○ **40g (1¾ oz) bread, without crusts**
- ○ **30ml (2 tbls) milk**
- ○ **15ml (1 tbls) chopped parsley**
- ○ **30g (1¼ oz) butter**
- ○ **100g (4 oz) fresh cream**
- ○ **1 chicken stock cube**
- ○ **250ml (9 fl oz) hot water**
- ○ **salt and pepper**
- ○ **pinch nutmeg**

1. Peel the onions and slice off the top quarter to hollow out the centre. Discard one-quarter of the cut-off section, finely chop the rest and put on one side. Grease a gratin dish with half the butter and arrange the onions on it.
2. Prepare the stuffing. Break the bread into pieces and soak in the milk; then mash it with a fork. Put the rest of the butter into a frying pan and lightly brown the chopped onion. Chop the salmon and the chicken very small. Mix the onions, salmon, chicken and bread together in a bowl. Add the parsley and blend in the egg. Add salt, pepper and nutmeg.
3. Set the oven to 205°C (400°F; gas mark 6). Fill the hollowed-out onions with the stuffing. Place on a gratin dish and dot with butter.
4. Dissolve the stock cube in boiling water and pour into the gratin dish. Cook for 50 minutes; 5 minutes before the end pour in the fresh cream. Serve very hot.

Oignons Farcis au Thon

Serves 4. Preparation: 20 min Cooking: 40 min

Onions Stuffed with Tuna

★ ★

- ○ **4 very large onions**
- ○ **1 tin 125g (5 oz) tuna fish**
- ○ **2 eggs**
- ○ **3 ripe tomatoes**
- ○ **15ml (1 tbls) chopped parsley**
- ○ **30ml (2 tbls) oil**
- ○ **10ml (2 tsp) breadcrumbs**
- ○ **250ml (9 fl oz) water**
- ○ **salt and pepper**

1. Peel the onions and cut them in half across. Hollow out the centres. Discard half the flesh and finely chop the remainder. Leave on one side.
2. Pour the oil into the bottom of a gratin dish. Arrange the onions in it.
3. Prepare the stuffing. Pour off the liquid from the tin of tuna, and mash the fish. Plunge the tomatoes into boiling water for 30 seconds, then drain them and cool them under the tap. Peel and cut in half to remove the seeds. Mash with a fork. Mix the tuna, tomatoes, eggs, chopped onion and chopped parsley together in a bowl. Add salt and pepper.
4. Set the oven at 205°C (400°F; gas mark 6).
5. Stuff the onions with the filling and scatter the tops with breadcrumbs. Pour the water into the dish.
6. Cook for 40 minutes, adding a little water to the dish if necessary, and serve immediately.

Cooking vegetables in a covered casserole can give marvellous results. Keep this method for new vegetables which have a delicate flavour, like carrots, turnips, peas, French beans, onions, lettuce hearts and chicory. Clean and wash them, then drain and arrange in a thick-based casserole that has been greased generously with butter. Add salt to accelerate the loss of the vegetables' natural juices – no other liquid, in fact, is used in the process. Cover the pan very tightly so that the steam condenses and falls back on to the vegetables; cook over a moderate heat throughout. If the heat is too low, the vegetables may disintegrate; if too high they may become caramelized and stick to the bottom of the pan. This method of cooking is slightly tricky so a certain amount of practice is needed. To minimize the risks the beginner can add 100ml (3½ fl oz) water to the bottom of the pan before starting.

Endives Sautées à la Crème (p44) ▶

Pommes de Terre au Lait et à la Crème

Potatoes with Milk and Cream

Serves 4.
Preparation: 10 min Cooking: 1 hr
★

- ○ **800g (1¾ lb) potatoes**
- ○ **½ litre (18 fl oz) milk**
- ○ **200g (7 oz) fresh cream**
- ○ **salt and pepper**

1. Choose long potatoes that will remain firm. Peel and wash, and slice across into rounds 3mm (⅛ inch) thick. Wipe them and sprinkle with salt and ground pepper.
2. Boil the milk in a saucepan, throw in the potatoes in small batches and bring to the boil again. Cover and leave to cook for 15 minutes over a very low heat.
3. At the end of this time, the potatoes should have absorbed all the milk. Add the cream and leave to cook over a low heat for 40 minutes more, half-covering the saucepan.

Serve these delicious boiled potatoes as they are or garnish them with herbs to accompany roast or braised meat. If you like you may serve them *au gratin*: pour into a greased dish, sprinkle with grated cheese and put under the grill or in a hot oven for 10 minutes until golden.

Purée aux Deux Fromages

Potato Purée with Two Kinds of Cheese

Serves 4. Preparation and cooking: 1 hr 10 min

- ○ **700g (1½ lb) potatoes**
- ○ **100g (4 oz) sausagemeat**
- ○ **150g (6 oz) tomme de Savoie cheese**
- ○ **50g (2 oz) grated Gruyère cheese**
- ○ **3 eggs**
- ○ **15ml (1 tbls) breadcrumbs**
- ○ **50g (2 oz) butter**
- ○ **salt and pepper**
- ○ **pinch nutmeg**

1. Wash the potatoes but do not peel them. Put in a large saucepan and cover with cold water. Bring to the boil, add salt, and simmer gently for about 20 minutes (test with the point of a knife to see if they are cooked).
2. Meanwhile, mash the sausagemeat with a fork. Dice the tomme de Savoie and mix with the sausagemeat. Add the grated Gruyère cheese.
3. When the potatoes are cooked, drain and leave on one side to cool. When you can handle them, peel them and grate them over the dish. Mix everything together very well, and beat in the eggs. Add salt, pepper and nutmeg, and mix again.
4. Set the oven at 205°C (400°F; gas mark 6).
5. Grease a mould or soufflé dish with 20g (¾ oz) butter and scatter it with breadcrumbs. Pour in the mixture and dot with knobs of butter. Cook for 30 minutes and serve hot.

It is helpful, if cooking chips, to have a deep fryer with a thermostat, or else you can buy a thermometer that you can plunge into the pan while the oil is heating up. Peel, wash and wipe the potatoes, and cut them into sticks 1cm (½ inch) thick for chips or 3mm (⅛ inch) thick for allumettes. Put the potatoes in a frying basket. Heat the oil to 170°C and plunge the basket into the boiling oil. Leave the chips to cook for 5 minutes, then drain and leave to cool. Bring the oil back to a temperature of 170°C (it will have fallen to about 150°C) and plunge the chips in a second time, for 3 to 5 minutes according to their thickness and their quality. When they have browned, drain them, sprinkle with salt and serve immediately.

What happens when you cook chips this way? On first coming into contact with the oil an impenetrable skin forms around each chip which seals in almost all the moisture. At the end of this first immersion, the chip is virtually cooked. When it is plunged in the second time, the outside layer becomes crisp and golden; at the same time the chip is puffed up by the water trapped inside. Make sure the oil never smokes and never reaches 180°C. At this temperature even the purest of oils decomposes, smokes and becomes toxic.

Pommes de Terre Surprise

Serves 4. Preparation and cooking: 1 hr

Potato Surprise with Mushrooms and Tomato Sauce

★★★

- ○ **600g (1 lb 5 oz) potatoes**
- ○ **2 eggs**
- ○ **60ml (4 tbls) flour**
- ○ **300g (11 oz) button mushrooms**
- ○ **15ml (1 tbls) chopped parsley**
- ○ **1 garlic clove**
- ○ **1 small tin pure tomato sauce**
- ○ **30ml (2 tbls) breadcrumbs**
- ○ **45ml (3 tbls) oil**
- ○ **20g (1 oz) butter**
- ○ **salt and pepper**

1. Wash the potatoes, but do not peel. Place in a large saucepan and cover amply with water. Bring to the boil, add salt and simmer gently for about 20 minutes. Prick with the point of a knife to see if they are ready.
2. Meanwhile, peel and chop the garlic finely. Trim and wipe the mushrooms, and slice finely.
3. Heat the oil in a frying pan and put in the mushrooms, garlic and parsley. Add the tomato sauce, salt and pepper. Cook for about 10 minutes, stirring frequently.
4. When the potatoes are cooked, strain and leave to cool. Then peel. Pass them through a sieve or blender. Pour the purée into a bowl, and add the eggs and the flour. Work the mixture well until you have a smooth paste.
5. Set the oven to 205°C (400°F; gas mark 6).
6. Shape the paste into balls about the size of an average potato. Hollow each one and fill with 15ml (1 tbls) of the mushroom and tomato sauce. Close over the hole and roll the potato ball in breadcrumbs.
7. Butter a gratin dish and arrange the potato balls on it. Cook in the oven for 20 minutes and serve hot.

Vermicelles de Pommes de Terre

Serves 4. Preparation: 15 min Cooking: 20 min

Potato Vermicelli

★

- ○ **600g (1 lb 5 oz) potatoes**
- ○ **60ml (4 tbls) oil**
- ○ **50g (2 oz) butter**
- ○ **salt**

1. Choose potatoes that will remain firm during cooking. Peel, wash and wipe them.
2. To prevent discoloration, grate them just before cooking, using a cylindrical hand grater or an electric mincer on the finest blade. The result will look rather like vermicelli. Place in a bowl and add salt.
3. Heat the oil in a large frying pan, add the butter and put in 2 or 3 tablespoonfuls of the potatoes. Flatten them with the back of the spoon into small fritters 0.5cm (1/6 inch) thick; brown them on one side, then turn them over and brown the other side. They should be very crunchy on the outside but soft in the middle. Cook on a fairly high heat to seal them for 6 to 8 minutes. Cooking time will depend on the thickness and the quality of the potatoes.
4. When the first rissoles are ready place them on a plate covered with kitchen paper and keep them warm while the rest are cooked.

These delicious rissoles can be served with all kinds of meat and poultry. The oil and butter may be replaced by goose fat, and the grated potatoes can be mixed with grated truffles.

Pommes de Terre Farcies au Thon

Potatoes Stuffed with Tuna

Serves 4.
Preparation and cooking: 45 min
★★

○ **4 large potatoes**
○ **1 tin 200g (8 oz) tuna**
○ **100g (4 oz) pitted green olives**
○ **8 anchovy fillets, canned**
○ **30ml (2 tbls) tomato ketchup**
○ **yolks of 2 hard-boiled eggs**
○ **salt and pepper**

1. Wash the potatoes and peel them. Place in a large saucepan, cover with cold water and bring to the boil. Add salt. Simmer gently for about 20 minutes until the potatoes are cooked.
2. Meanwhile, mash the tuna fish with a fork and roughly chop the olives and 4 of the anchovy fillets. Keep back 4 olives and 4 anchovies for garnishing. Put the egg yolks in a bowl and mash them. Mix in the tuna, olives, ketchup and chopped anchovies. Add very little salt, and pepper.
3. When the potatoes are cooked, strain them and leave to cool. Hollow out their centres. Discard half the flesh and purée the rest. Add this purée to the mixture and check the seasoning.
4. Set the oven at 230°C (450°F; gas mark 8). Grease a gratin dish.
5. Stuff the potatoes with the mixture and garnish each one with a green olive wrapped in an anchovy fillet. Arrange the potatoes on the dish and put it in the oven for 5 minutes to heat them through.

Gâteau de Pommes de Terre

Potato Gâteau

Serves 4-6. Preparation: 20 min Cooking: 45 min

★★★

○ **1kg (2¼ lb) potatoes**
○ **125g (5 oz) butter**
○ **salt and pepper**

1. Choose long potatoes that remain firm during cooking. Peel and wash them, and slice across very finely into rounds 1mm (⅛ inch) thick (use an electric slicer if possible). Wash again until the water runs clear, so that all the starch is removed, then drain and wipe. Put in a bowl and sprinkle with salt and pepper. Mix well to distribute the seasoning evenly.
2. Put 25g (1 oz) butter on one side and melt the rest in a small saucepan. Pour over the potatoes and mix quickly making sure that every slice is coated.
3. Set the oven at 220°C (425°F; gas mark 7). With the 25g (1 oz) butter remaining, grease the base and sides of a mould or soufflé dish large enough to hold all the potatoes. Cover the bottom with a layer of potatoes arranged in overlapping circles, then line the sides in the same fashion. Continue like this until all the potatoes have been used up, but do not make more than six layers.
4. Put the cake into the oven for about 45 minutes. Check with the point of a knife to see if ready: it should pierce the potatoes easily. If it does not, continue cooking for a few minutes more.
5. Turn the cake out on to a serving dish. It should have a golden crust. Serve immediately.

This potato gâteau is a feast for the eyes and for the palate. It goes very well with all kinds of meat, but would be absolutely perfect with a large roast such as leg of lamb or rib of beef. For a really special occasion intersperse slices of truffle between the layers of potato. The butter in the recipe may be replaced by goose or duck fat.

Gratin Dauphinois

Serves 4. Preparation: 15 min Cooking: 1 hr 20 min

Potatoes Dauphinois, Baked with Cheese

★ ★

○ **1kg (2¼ lb) potatoes**
○ **½ litre (18 fl oz) milk**
○ **100g (4 oz) fresh cream**
○ **1 garlic clove**
○ **50g (2 oz) butter**
○ **salt and pepper**
○ **pinch nutmeg**

1. Peel and wash the potatoes; cut into thin rounds. Put in a bowl and add salt, pepper and grated nutmeg, mixing well to distribute the seasoning evenly.
2. Peel the garlic clove. Rub the surface of an earthenware oven dish with garlic, then grease with 20g (1 oz) butter. If this recipe is to succeed, the dish must be 6-7cm (2½ inches-3 inches) deep and the potato layer not more than 5cm (2 inches) deep.
3. Set the oven at 187°C (362°F; gas mark 4½). Mix the cream and the milk.
4. Layer the potatoes in the dish and pour the cream and milk over, so that they are just covered. If not, add a little more milk. Dot the top with knobs of butter.
5. Put the dish in the oven for about 1 hour 30 minutes. At the end of cooking the potatoes should be deliciously melting (*fondant*).
6. Serve this dish very hot. Place under the grill for 5 minutes just before serving to crisp the top.

This tasty way of cooking potatoes makes them the ideal partner for all kinds of roast meat, and for chicken and other poultry.

Croquettes au Fromage

Serves 4. Preparation and cooking: 1 hr

Potato and Cheese Croquettes

★ ★ ★

○ **800g (1¾ lb) potatoes**
○ **60g (2½ oz) grated Gruyère cheese**
○ **200g (7 oz) Mozzarella cheese**
○ **100g (4 oz) Mortadella sausage**
○ **3 eggs**
○ **100g (4 oz) white breadcrumbs**
○ **oil for frying**
○ **salt and pepper**
○ **pinch nutmeg**

1. Wash the potatoes but do not peel them. Place in a large saucepan and cover with cold water. Bring to the boil, then add salt. Simmer gently for about 30 minutes (test for readiness with the point of a knife). Strain, leave to cool and peel; then put through a sieve or blender to make a purée.
2. Cut the Mortadella into strips, dice the Mozzarella about 2cm (¾ inch) square.
3. Put the purée in a bowl with the eggs and grated cheese. Add salt, pepper and nutmeg and mix well. Shape into croquettes about the size of a small egg, hollow out the centre and insert a strip of Mortadella and some Mozzarella. Close up the hole and roll the croquette in breadcrumbs.
4. Heat the oil in a frying pan and lightly brown the croquettes. Serve hot.

Potatoes come in so many varieties that they can be used in countless different ways, right through the year. Try to choose a quality of potato suitable for the recipe you are following. Potatoes to be boiled or steamed or used in gratins and salads should have a firm, waxy flesh that will not disintegrate in cooking. For soups and broths, purées and chips choose a more floury type of potato.

Pommes Dentelle

Serves 4. Preparation: 15 min Cooking: 20 min

Lacy Potato Cakes (Dentelles)

★★

○ **600g (1 lb 5 oz) potatoes**
○ **50g (2 oz) butter, oil or goose fat**
○ **salt**

1. This recipe really does require firm, waxy potatoes. Peel, wash and wipe the potatoes in a cloth.
2. At the last minute slice the potatoes as finely as possible, as if you were making crisps (use an electric slicer if possible). Put the slices in a bowl.
3. Heat 20g (1 oz) butter, oil or goose fat in a frying pan. With a large spoon add the potato slices, a few at a time, and spread them out into a thin layer so that not more than 3 or 4 are overlapping.
4. Over a moderate heat lightly brown the potato cake on one side, then with a spatula, turn it over to brown on the other; 5 or 6 minutes in all.
5. Place on a plate and keep hot while the next potato cakes are cooking. By using two frying pans you can cook two potato cakes at a time. Add salt at the end of cooking. The potato cakes should be so thin that the pattern on the plate is visible through them. To avoid breaking them, use a small non-stick pan, at most 22cm (8½ inches) in diameter. You can of course make them thicker, but the pan should be covered as soon as the first side is golden to speed up the cooking.

These potato cakes have a very delicate flavour and can be used to accompany any roast meat or casserole.

Tentation de Jansson

Serves 4. Preparation: 30 min Cooking: 1 hr approx

Jansson's Potatoes with Cream and Anchovies

★★

○ **1kg (2¼ lb) medium-sized potatoes**
○ **3 large onions**
○ **16 fillets marinated Norwegian anchovies**
○ **150g (6 oz) fresh cream**
○ **100ml (3½ fl oz) milk**
○ **80g (3¼ oz) butter**
○ **30ml (2 tbls) white breadcrumbs**
○ **salt and pepper**

1. Peel the onions and chop them finely.
2. Melt 50g (2 oz) butter in a frying pan and lightly brown the onions over a very low heat.
3. Peel the potatoes, wash and slice.
4. Set the oven at 205°C (400°F; gas mark 6). Grease a gratin dish with 20g (1 oz) butter and put in a layer of potatoes, then a layer of onions, and a layer of anchovies. Continue until all the ingredients are used up, finishing with a layer of potatoes.
5. Heat the milk in a saucepan, add the fresh cream and bring to the boil. Add salt and pepper. Pour this mixture over the potatoes. Sprinkle with breadcrumbs and dot with knobs of butter.
6. Put in the oven for 1 hour. Serve hot.

If no Norwegian anchovies, which are preserved in a slightly sweet brine are available, use salted anchovies instead.

If you have any vegetable purée to use up, you can always make a gratin or better still, a soufflé or pie, following the recipe for Soufflé of Artichoke Hearts or for Baked Pumpkin. If there is a great deal left over, you can mix with another vegetable. Certain combinations are especially delicious: pumpkin-celery; cauliflower-French beans; peas-spinach.

Petits Pois Frais au Lard

Serves 4. Preparation: 15 min Cooking: 30 min

Fresh Green Peas with Bacon

★

○ 1kg (2¼ lb) unshelled peas
○ 100g (4 oz) smoked bacon
○ 1 onion
○ 25g (1 oz) butter
○ 1 stock cube
○ 250ml (9 fl oz) hot water
○ salt and pepper
○ 1 small red pepper (optional)

1. Shell the peas. Peel the onion and chop well. Cut the bacon into thin sticks. Wash the red pepper, cut in two to remove the seeds, and slice thinly.
2. Melt the butter in the frying pan and lightly brown the onions and bacon over a very low heat.
3. Dissolve the stock cube in hot water and pour into the pan. Season. Add the peas and the red pepper, and cook for about 20 minutes until the peas are tender. Serve hot.

Purée de Petits Pois

Serves 4. Preparation and cooking: 20 min

Purée of Peas

★★

○ 1 large packet 1kg (2¼ lb) frozen peas
○ 30ml (2 tbls) fresh cream
○ 50g (2 oz) butter
○ 2.5ml (½ tsp) granulated sugar
○ salt and pepper

1. Cook the peas according to the instructions.
2. When they are cooked, pass through a sieve or blender to purée, making sure that all the skins are removed.
3. Put the purée into a saucepan over a very low heat, add the butter and the cream, stirring constantly with a wooden spoon to prevent the bottom from burning. Add sugar, salt and pepper and serve immediately.

This delicate purée perfectly accompanies all game birds and roast poultry.

Jardinière d'Avril

Serves 4. Preparation: 20 min Cooking: 45 min approx

Casserole of Spring Vegetables

★★

○ 500g (1 lb 2 oz) unshelled peas
○ 250g (9 oz) small new carrots
○ 250g (9 oz) new turnips
○ 20 small white onions, or large spring onions
○ 1 small lettuce
○ 15ml (1 tbls) oil
○ 80g (3¼ oz) butter
○ 2.5ml (½ tsp) granulated sugar
○ 100ml (3½ fl oz) water
○ salt

1. Shell the peas. Peel the onions. Remove the outer leaves of the lettuce, wash and quarter. Scrape the carrots, wash them and cut into 4 lengthways. Peel, wash and dice the turnips into cubes 1cm (¼ inch) square. Put the vegetables on one side, keeping separate.
2. Heat the oil in a thick pan, then add the butter. As soon as it has melted, add the onions and the carrots. Sweat for about 10 minutes over a low heat without allowing them to brown, then add the lettuce and let it cook for 3 minutes before adding the peas and turnips. Season with salt and sugar and mix all together well.
3. Add the water to the pan. Cover, and leave to cook over a low heat without interruption for 30 minutes.
4. At the end of this time, remove the lid. The vegetables should be cooked, but not overcooked – slightly crunchy. If any liquid remains in the pan, increase the heat and reduce it for several minutes, without a lid.

This delicious spring casserole goes with all grilled or roast meat.

To make Potatoes Savoyard, follow the recipe for Potatoes Dauphinois, but omit the garlic. Replace the milk and cream with chicken stock and sprinkle each layer of potatoes with grated Gruyère cheese.

Pois Chiches à la Paysanne

Serves 4. Preparation: 10 min Cooking: 2 hr 20 min

Chickpeas Peasant-Style

★

○ **500g (1 lb 2 oz) chickpeas**
○ **1 large onion**
○ **250g (9 oz) smoked bacon**
○ **500g (1 lb 2 oz) potatoes**
○ **salt and pepper**

Bouquet garni:
○ **5 sprigs parsley**
○ **1 bay leaf**
○ **1 sprig thyme**
○ **3 cloves**

1. The day before: put the chickpeas to soak in a large pan of cold water.
2. The next day cut the bacon into sticks, peel the onion and spike it with the cloves. Tie the bouquet garni together.
3. Drain the chickpeas and put them into a heavy pan. Cover well with cold water and add the bouquet garni, the onion and the bacon. Allow to cook, covered, for 2 hours on a low heat.
4. At the end of this time, remove the bouquet garni and the onion. Peel, wash, and quarter the potatoes. Add to the pan and season. Cook for a further 20 minutes and serve very hot.

Pois Chiches à la Milanaise

Serves 4. Preparation: 15 min Cooking: 2 hr 20 min

Chickpeas Milanese

★ ★

○ **300g (11 oz) chickpeas**
○ **100g (4 oz) smoked bacon**
○ **1 onion**
○ **1 carrot**
○ **1 celery heart**
○ **1 garlic clove**
○ **200g (8 oz) pork fat**
○ **50g (2 oz) grated Parmesan or Gruyère cheese**
○ **12 slices toast**

Bouquet garni:
○ **1 sprig thyme**
○ **1 bay leaf**
○ **10 sprigs parsley**

1. The day before: put the chickpeas to soak in a large pan of cold water.
2. The following day cut the bacon into sticks, chop the garlic, cut the pork fat into pieces about 3cm (1 inch) long by 2cm (¾ inch) wide. Peel and wash the carrot, onion and celery.
3. Put the bacon into a heavy pan together with the onion, celery, garlic, bouquet garni and pork fat. Cover with water. Add salt and cook for 30 minutes, then leave to cool.
4. Drain the chickpeas, then add them to the pan. Add 2 litres (3½ pints) of water, and cover.
5. Cook over a low heat for 2 hours. Serve hot with toast and grated cheese.

Pois Chiches aux Travers de Porc

Serves 4.
Preparation and cooking: 2 hr 10 min
★ ★

Chickpeas with Pork Ribs

○ **500g (1 lb 2 oz) chickpeas**
○ **500g (1 lb 2 oz) ribs of pork**
○ **1 thick rasher 50g (2 oz) smoked bacon**
○ **2.5ml (½ tsp) rosemary**
○ **4 sage leaves**
○ **2 peeled garlic cloves**
○ **60ml (4 tbls) oil**
○ **salt and pepper**

1. The day before: put the chickpeas to soak in a large pan of cold water.
2. The following day drain the chickpeas and put them in a large saucepan with the pork ribs, half the rosemary, 2 sage leaves and 1 garlic clove. Cover with cold water. Add salt and cook for 1 hour 30 minutes by simmering slowly.
3. 15 minutes before the end, cut the rasher of bacon into four. Pour the oil into the pan, add the bacon and brown it lightly. Add the second garlic clove, the rest of the sage and the rosemary, and brown everything lightly.
4. When the chickpeas and pork are cooked, drain them, reserving 200ml (7 fl oz) of the stock.
5. Add the chickpeas and the pork to the pan, pour in stock, and season. Leave to cook for 30 minutes over a low heat. Serve hot.

Poivrons comme à Sorrente

Serves 4. Preparation and cooking: 1 hr 15 min

Peppers Stuffed with Mozzarella

★ ★ ★

○ **4 plump red peppers**
○ **200g (8 oz) Mozzarella cheese**
○ **25g (1 oz) butter**
○ **3 ripe tomatoes**
○ **1 egg**
○ **30ml (2 tbls) white breadcrumbs**
○ **salt and pepper**
○ **oil for frying**

1. Wash and wipe the peppers, and place under a very hot grill. Cook for about 20 minutes, turning them often, until the skin is completely black. Then put them in a saucepan with a tight cover, and leave to cool. This makes them easy to peel.
2. When they are cool, strip off their skins, cut in half and remove the seeds. Divide the Mozzarella into 8 pieces, adding salt and pepper to each. Put one piece into each pepper half; roll the edges over and secure with a cocktail stick.
3. Beat the egg well and add salt. Put the breadcrumbs on a plate. Dip each rolled-up pepper into the egg, and then into the breadcrumbs.
4. Heat the oil in a frying pan, brown the peppers lightly and drain on kitchen paper.
5. Wash and quarter the tomatoes, put through a sieve or blender. Melt the butter in a pan and add the tomato pulp. Season, and cook for 5 minutes.
6. Add the peppers to the tomato sauce and leave to simmer for 10 minutes over a very low heat. Serve immediately.

Poivrons Grillés

Serves 4. Preparation and cooking: 50 min approx

Grilled Peppers

★

○ **6 plump red peppers**
○ **3 garlic cloves**
○ **150ml (5 fl oz) olive oil**
○ **salt**

1. Set the grill at its highest.
2. Wash the peppers, and cook under the grill for about 20 minutes, turning frequently until the skin is completely black. Then put in a tightly sealed saucepan and leave to cool.
3. When the peppers are cool, peel off their skins, cut them open to remove their seeds, then cut them lengthways into strips about 2cm (¾ inch) wide.
4. Peel and finely slice the garlic. Layer the peppers in a bowl, placing several slices of garlic between each layer. Add salt and sprinkle with oil.
5. Serve these peppers warm or very cold.

You can use green or yellow peppers, or mix the colours. If they are served cold, garnish with anchovies and parsley.

Some vegetables are delicious grilled. Grill tomatoes, mushrooms, aubergines, peppers and onions over charcoal with meat and poultry cooked in the same way. Grilling is the oldest method of cooking known to man. Once cooked, the vegetables may be seasoned with a sprinkling of olive oil and lemon juice, and with salt and pepper.

Poivrons Farcis au Fromage

Serves 4. Preparation and cooking: 1 hr approx

Stuffed Peppers with Cheese Sauce ★★

○ **4 large peppers**
○ **5ml (1 tsp) anchovy paste**
○ **100g (4 oz) fresh cream**
○ **100g (4 oz) grated Gruyère cheese**
○ **30ml (2 tbls) vodka, gin or aquavit**
○ **30g (1¼ oz) butter**
○ **15ml (1 tbls) flour**
○ **salt and pepper**
○ **pinch nutmeg**

1. Wash the peppers. Slice off the top quarter and remove the seeds.
2. Melt the butter in a saucepan, add the flour, stirring constantly, then the anchovy paste, fresh cream and spirit. Continue to stir for 5 minutes. Blend in the cheese. Season with salt, pepper and nutmeg. Cook over a low heat for 10 minutes, then leave to cool.
3. Set the oven at 205°C (400°F; gas mark 6). Oil a gratin dish.
4. Fill the peppers with the cheese sauce and arrange in the dish. Cook for 40 minutes and serve hot.

Poivrons Braisés aux Câpres

Serves 4. Preparation: 10 min Cooking: 40 min

Braised Peppers with Capers ★

○ **1.5kg (3¼ lb) red and green peppers**
○ **60g (2½ oz) capers**
○ **8 anchovy fillets, canned**
○ **150ml (5 fl oz) oil**
○ **50g (2 oz) stale bread**
○ **pepper**

1. Wash and quarter the peppers, removing the seeds and stalk, then cut each quarter into 3 pieces. Drain the capers and chop the anchovies.
2. Heat the oil in a heavy pan and brown the peppers lightly, turning them often. Add the anchovies and capers. Cover and cook for 30 minutes over a very low heat, stirring now and then.
3. When the peppers are cooked, grate the bread and add the breadcrumbs to the peppers. Mix in well and remove from the heat. Season with pepper.
4. Serve hot, warm or cold.

These peppers can be served on their own, or as an accompaniment to roast pork or veal, or grilled or fried fresh tuna fish.

Poivrons Farcis au Jambon

Serves 4. Preparation: 20 min Cooking: 40 min

Peppers Stuffed with Ham ★★

○ **4 red or green peppers**
○ **150g (6 oz) cooked ham**
○ **100g (4 oz) sausagemeat**
○ **2 eggs**
○ **2 large ripe tomatoes**
○ **50g (2 oz) stale bread**
○ **50g (2 oz) grated Gruyère cheese**
○ **60ml (4 tbls) breadcrumbs**
○ **15ml (1 tbls) oil**
○ **salt and pepper**
○ **pinch nutmeg**

1. Wash the peppers, and slice off the top quarter, discarding the cap and seeds. Chop the ham. Grate the bread. Plunge the tomatoes into boiling water for 30 seconds, then drain them and hold under cold running water; peel. Cut the tomatoes in half to remove the seeds, and mash roughly with a fork.
2. Mash the sausagemeat in a bowl and add the ham and the tomatoes. Then blend in the eggs and add half the breadcrumbs and 30ml (2 tbls) of grated cheese. Season with salt and a little pepper. Add the nutmeg and stir together well.
3. Set the oven at 205°C (400°F; gas mark 6). Oil a gratin dish.
4. Stuff the peppers with the filling and sprinkle with the rest of the cheese, then the breadcrumbs. Arrange on the dish and cook for 40 minutes. Serve them hot, or very cold.

To enjoy vegetables croques-au-sel, *steep them in coarse sea salt with a pinch of paprika added, which gives them a pleasant pink colour. Serve them with thick slices of bread and butter.*

Poireaux au Gratin
Gratin of Leeks with Ham

Serves 4. Preparation and cooking: 1 hr

★★

- ○ **12 leeks**
- ○ **12 thin slices smoked bacon, or cooked ham**
- ○ **50g (2 oz) butter**
- ○ **2 eggs**
- ○ **250ml (9 fl oz) milk**
- ○ **50g (2 oz) grated Gruyère cheese**
- ○ **100g (4 oz) fresh cream**
- ○ **2.5ml (½ tsp) sugar**
- ○ **salt and pepper**
- ○ **pinch nutmeg**

1. Clean and wash the leeks, discarding three-quarters of the green part. Add salt, sugar, a little grated nutmeg and ground pepper to some boiling water in a large saucepan. Blanch the leeks in this for 10 minutes.
2. At the end of this time, drain the leeks and leave them to cool. Roll a slice of the bacon or ham around each one.
3. Set the oven at 220°C (425°F; gas mark 7). Grease an oven dish with 25g (1 oz) butter and arrange the leeks along it lengthways.
4. Beat the eggs well in a bowl, add the cream, milk and cheese. Season with salt, pepper and nutmeg and mix together well. Pour this mixture on the leeks and dot with knobs of butter.
5. Put the dish in the oven for about 20 minutes until the top is golden. Serve very hot from the cooking dish.

Poireaux à la Pizzaiola
Leeks with Tomatoes and Cheese

Serves 4. Preparation and cooking: 45 min

★★

- ○ **1kg (2¼ lb) leeks**
- ○ **500g (1 lb 2 oz) ripe tomatoes**
- ○ **100g (4 oz) cooked ham**
- ○ **100g (4 oz) Emmenthal cheese**
- ○ **5ml (1 tsp) marjoram**
- ○ **90ml (6 tbls) olive oil**
- ○ **salt and pepper**

1. Clean the leeks, discarding three-quarters of the green part. Blanch the leeks in boiling, salted water for approximately 15 minutes. They should be cooked but still firm.
2. While the leeks are cooking, quarter the tomatoes and put them through a sieve or blender to purée.
3. Strain the leeks in a colander. Slice the ham and the Emmenthal finely.
4. Heat 30ml (2 tbls) olive oil in a saucepan, add the tomato purée and the marjoram. Season with salt and pepper and cook for 10 minutes over a high heat.
5. Set the oven at 230°C (450°F; gas mark 8).
6. Put 30ml (2 tbls) oil in a gratin dish and arrange in it a layer of leeks, a layer of ham, and a layer of tomato sauce. Trickle over 15ml (1 tbls) of oil, sprinkle with marjoram and grated cheese. Continue like this until all the ingredients have been used up, finishing with a layer of cheese and a few pinches of marjoram.
7. Place in the oven for 10 minutes and serve immediately.

Another way of cooking potatoes is to place them, unpeeled, in salted, simmering water. When they are almost cooked, pour away all the cooking water, and leave the saucepan to stand for 10 minutes over a very low heat; then serve. The potatoes will have dried out beautifully.

Potatoes baked in the ashes are delicious, but not always easy to make! Serve them with butter. If you like roast potatoes, it is worth trying this method. Cook them on the middle shelf of the oven, and carry them to the table between 2 napkins when ready, dressed with fresh butter, sea salt and ground pepper. Be sure to choose even-shaped floury potatoes for this.

Poireaux au Vin Rouge ou Blanc

Leeks with Red or White Wine

Serves 4. Preparation: 10 min
Cooking: 1 hr 45 min approx
★

○ **2kg (4½ lb) leeks**
○ **1 bottle red or white Bordeaux**
○ **80g (3¼ oz) butter**
○ **1 sprig thyme**
○ **½ bay leaf**
○ **salt and pepper**
○ **pinch nutmeg**

1. Clean the leeks, discarding three-quarters of the green part, and cut into pieces about 10cm (4 inches) long. Wash and drain in a colander.
2. Melt the butter in a heavy pan and cook the leeks over a low heat without browning them. Pour in wine. Add salt, pepper, thyme and the ½ bay leaf. Bring to the boil and cover. Cook for about 1 hour 30 minutes over a very low heat.

Serve the leeks very hot, with croûtons and poached eggs if you like.

Potiron Farci

Stuffed Pumpkin

Serves 4-6. Preparation and cooking: 1 hr 30 min

★★★

○ **1 good-sized pumpkin**
○ **800g (1¾ lb) veal**
○ **300g (11 oz) potatoes**
○ **1 stick celery**
○ **1 carrot**
○ **1 small onion**
○ **1 tin 400g (14 oz) peeled tomatoes**
○ **100ml (3½ fl oz) dry white wine**
○ **150g (6 oz) butter**
○ **30ml (2 tbls) flour**
○ **2 cloves**
○ **salt and pepper**

1. Cut a 'cap' off the pumpkin 3cm (1 inch) thick. Remove the seeds and scoop out the flesh with a spoon, leaving 1.5cm (½ inch) inside the skin. Put the flesh on one side.
2. Bring some salted water to the boil in a saucepan large enough to hold the pumpkin. Allow the pumpkin to simmer gently for about 30 minutes. Test by pricking with a fork to see if it is ready. When the pumpkin is tender, remove from the heat and drain upside down in a colander.
3. Meanwhile, peel and finely chop the onion. String the celery and peel the carrot, and slice finely. Cut the meat into cubes 4cm (1½ inches) square and sprinkle with flour.
4. Melt the butter in a heavy pan and brown the vegetables lightly. Add the meat and seal for about 5 minutes, turning with a wooden spoon to ensure that it browns equally all over. Then pour in the wine and allow it to evaporate over a high heat. Drain and reserve the juice from the tinned tomatoes; purée the tomatoes in a sieve or blender. Add all to the pan and season with salt, pepper and cloves. Cook over a low heat for 30 minutes stirring from time to time.
5. Meanwhile, peel and dice the potatoes. Cut the pumpkin flesh into cubes 2cm (¾ inch) square. Add these to the pan and cook, covered, for a further 30 minutes over a low heat.
6. 10 minutes before the end of this time, set the oven at 230°C (450°F; gas mark 8). Place the pumpkin on a dish and put in the oven for 5 minutes to allow it to dry out completely. Then arrange on a serving dish, fill it with the stuffing, and serve immediately.

Beef marrow lends an incomparable flavour to braised vegetables. Cook it with the vegetables, or poach it for 10 minutes in lightly simmering, salted water; then cut into fine rounds and arrange over the vegetables before serving. If the marrow is added directly to the vegetables, prepare it some hours beforehand by cutting into fine rounds 2cm (¾ inch) thick which you should plunge into iced, salted water and place in the refrigerator for at least 4 hours. Then drain, add to the blanched vegetables and continue braising them according to the recipe.

Soufflé de Potiron

Pumpkin Soufflé

Serves 4. Preparation and cooking: 1 hr 10 min

★★★

○ 1 800g (1¾ lb) slice of pumpkin
○ 50g (2 oz) grated Gruyère cheese
○ 3 eggs, separated
○ 70g (3 oz) butter
○ salt and sugar
○ pinch nutmeg
○ 15ml (1 tbls) sieved flour

1. Skin the pumpkin slice and remove the seeds. Dice the flesh into cubes 4cm (1½ inches) square.
2. Put the pumpkin cubes in a saucepan, add 2ml (½ tsp) of salt and the same amount of sugar. Barely cover with water. Bring to the boil, then lower the heat and leave to cook for 10 minutes, simmering gently.
3. At the end of this time, drain the pumpkin in a colander and purée it in a sieve or blender. Put this purée in a saucepan with 50g (2 oz) butter, add the flour, and cook over a gentle heat for 10 minutes, stirring all the time to prevent the bottom from scorching.
4. When the purée is well-blended and of an even consistency, remove from the heat and add the grated cheese, a little more salt, and a little grated nutmeg. Beat in the egg yolks one by one, incorporating them well.
5. Beat the egg whites stiffly and fold carefully into the mixture. Set the oven at 187°C (350°F; gas mark 4½).
6. With the remaining butter, grease a soufflé dish large enough to hold one and a half times the quantity of the soufflé mixture. Pour into the dish; the dish should be only three-quarters full.
7. Cook the soufflé for 25 minutes in the oven, and serve immediately.

Flan de Potiron

Baked Pumpkin

Serves 4. Preparation and cooking: 1 hr 10 min

★★

○ 1 1kg (2¼ lb) slice of pumpkin
○ 125g (5 oz) butter
○ 250ml (9 fl oz) milk
○ 4 eggs
○ 100g (4 oz) grated Gruyère cheese
○ salt and pepper
○ pinch nutmeg

1. Skin the pumpkin and remove the seeds. Cut into cubes 3cm (1 inch) square.
2. Melt 50g (2 oz) butter in a pan and lightly brown the pumpkin. Add the milk and cook over a low heat until the pumpkin is tender, for about 15 minutes.
3. When the pumpkin is tender, pass through a sieve or blender to purée. Add 50g (2 oz) butter and the grated cheese to the purée in a bowl, and season with salt, pepper and nutmeg. Mix all together well.
4. Set the oven at 180°C (350°F; gas mark 4). Beat the eggs well and fold into the mixture carefully. With the remaining butter grease a soufflé mould and pour in the mixture. Place in the oven for 40 minutes.
5. Serve hot, warm or cold.

A mirepoix is a mixture of vegetables invented in the nineteenth century by a nobleman who gave it his name. It usually includes carrots, celery, mushrooms, shallots and onions, cut into very small cubes and seasoned with aromatic herbs, all lightly sealed in butter. Sometimes small cubes of raw ham are added. It is used to thicken the gravy of braised meat or vegetables, and of roast meat.

A mirepoix should not be confused with julienne vegetables. These very fine sticks – between 1mm (⅛ inch) and 1.5cm (½ inch) thick and 4cm (1½ inches) long – are of ham, cooked chicken, orange and lemon peel, and all kinds of vegetables, such as carrots, celery, leeks, mushrooms. A special slicer called a mouli julienne facilitates their preparation.

Poireaux à la Pizzaiola (p72) ▶

Scaroles Braisées aux Poireaux

Serves 4. Preparation: 10 min Cooking: 25 min

Braised Endives with Leeks

★

○ **2 endives**
○ **6 medium-sized leeks**
○ **60g (2½ oz) butter**
○ **1 stock cube**
○ **100ml (3½ fl oz) hot water**
○ **salt and pepper**

1. Pull apart the leaves of the endives and wash them with plenty of water. Clean the leeks: you should keep most of the green part. Slice both vegetables finely.
2. Melt the butter in a pan, add the vegetables and cook them for 10 minutes over a low heat. Season.
3. Dissolve the stock cube in boiling water and pour into the pan. Cook covered for 15 minutes.
4. At the end of this time, if too much juice remains, reduce over a high heat, stirring all the time. Serve hot.

These braised endives are very good served with boiled or grilled meat.

Laitues Braisées à la Moelle

Serves 4. Preparation: 15 min Cooking: 20 min

Braised Lettuces with Marrow

★ ★

○ **4 good-sized lettuces**
○ **100g (4 oz) beef marrow**
○ **60g (2½ oz) butter**
○ **salt and pepper**

1. The day before: cut the marrow into slices 0.5cm (⅛ inch) thick, put in a lightly salted bowl of water and leave in the refrigerator overnight.
2. The next day wash the lettuces whole, discarding any withered leaves. Plunge into boiling, salted water for 3 minutes. Drain in a colander, pressing on them lightly to squeeze out all the water.
3. Set the oven at 205°C (400°F; gas mark 6). Grease a gratin dish with 30g (1¼ oz) butter. Drain the slices of marrow.
4. Gently open out the lettuce leaves, without separating, and season the hearts with salt and pepper. Slip a slice of beef marrow between each leaf and close the lettuces up.
5. Arrange the lettuces on the gratin dish and dot with knobs of butter. Cover the dish with a sheet of greaseproof paper or foil.
6. Place in the oven for 20 minutes, remove the cover and serve straight away.

Fairly difficult to find today are Japanese artichokes, which resemble corkscrews and are covered with a light-brown skin, like a new potato. These roots, originally from Japan, were not cultivated in France until 1882. Their taste is similar to salsify but they are much more tender. If you do manage to get some, wash them and cut off both ends, then put them in a cloth with 2 large handfuls of coarse salt. Roll the cloth round them and twist from left to right and back again. This movement enables the coarse salt grains to rub the peel off. Then wash again, and blanch for 10 minutes in boiling salted water to prevent discoloration during cooking. Strain and sauté in butter in a frying pan for 10 to 15 minutes. Sprinkle with salt, pepper, parsley or chopped herbs before serving. They can also be served with a cream sauce or baked in the oven with a béchamel sauce and grated Gruyère cheese.

Feuilles de Laitues Farcies

Serves 4. Preparation and cooking: 1 hr 20 min

Stuffed Lettuce Leaves

★★★

○ **2 good-sized lettuces**
○ **100g (4 oz) sausagemeat**
○ **250g (9 oz) cooked veal**
○ **10 sprigs parsley**
○ **1 garlic clove**
○ **1 egg**
○ **1 medium-sized onion**
○ **15ml (1 tbls) breadcrumbs**
○ **15ml (1 tbls) tomato concentrate**
○ **15ml (1 tbls) chopped parsley**
○ **100g (4 oz) grated Parmesan or Gruyère cheese**
○ **1 stock cube**
○ **250ml (9 fl oz) hot water**
○ **60g (2½ oz) butter**
○ **salt and pepper**

1. Discard any withered lettuce leaves. Separate and wash the rest, then plunge into boiling, salted water for 2 minutes. Drain, hold under a cold running tap, and drain again. Reserve the 12 largest leaves. Chop the hearts and smaller leaves.
2. Peel and chop the garlic. Melt 30g (1¼ oz) butter in a pan and lightly brown the garlic and chopped parsley. Chop the veal well and add it to the pan with the sausagemeat which has been mashed with a fork. Add the chopped lettuce and cook for 5 minutes.
3. Dissolve the stock cube in hot water and pour half into the pan. Simmer until the liquid has evaporated, then add the breadcrumbs. Mix in well, remove from the heat and leave to cool. Season.
4. Beat the egg well and stir into the mixture. Add the cheese and mix everything together again.
5. Place the stuffing inside the 12 lettuce leaves you have reserved; fold them into 4 and tie with kitchen thread.
6. Peel and chop the onion well. In a pan, melt the rest of the butter, add the onion and brown it lightly over a very low heat. Add the lettuce parcels and brown them lightly all over. Dilute the tomato concentrate in the rest of the stock and pour into the pan. Cook for another 20 minutes uncovered over a very low heat. Serve very hot.

Salsifis Sautés au Beurre

Serves 4. Preparation: 15 min Cooking: 1 hr approx

Salsify Sautéed in Butter

★

○ **1kg (2¼ lb) salsify**
○ **15ml (1 tbls) flour**
○ **1 lemon**
○ **15ml (1 tbls) coarse salt**
○ **2 litres (3½ pints) water**
○ **80g (2½ oz) butter**
○ **15ml (1 tbls) chopped herbs**
○ **salt and pepper**

1. Squeeze the lemon and keep one half. Mix the flour with cold water, add the coarse salt and lemon juice and bring to the boil in a saucepan.
2. Peel the salsify. Cut into pieces 6cm (2¾ inches) long and rub each piece with the half lemon to prevent discoloration.
3. Add the salsify to the water boiling in the saucepan. Simmer gently for 45 minutes until it is tender, but not soft. Test by piercing with a fork; if the prongs do not enter easily, continue cooking for a few more minutes before straining.
4. Melt the butter in a frying pan and sauté the salsify for 10 to 15 minutes, turning the pieces often to brown them evenly on all sides. Add salt and pepper. Sprinkle with herbs and serve immediately.

The butter can be replaced with the juices from a roast: cook the salsify in them, covered, for 10 minutes. The butter can also be replaced with 250g (9 oz) fresh cream which should be reduced by half before taking the salsify off the heat and seasoning with pepper and nutmeg. Then serve with a knob of butter if desired.

Tomates Farcies au Riz

Tomatoes Stuffed with Rice

Serves 4. Preparation and cooking: 50 min

★★

- ○ **8 large tomatoes**
- ○ **40g (1¾ oz) butter**
- ○ **120ml (8 tbls) rice**
- ○ **1 garlic clove, chopped small**
- ○ **15ml (1 tbls) chopped parsley**
- ○ **50g (2 oz) grated Gruyère cheese**
- ○ **15ml (1 tbls) oil**
- ○ **salt and pepper**

1. Wash the tomatoes and slice off across one-quarter of the way from the top. Hollow out the centre with a small spoon and reserve the flesh. Salt the inside of the tomatoes and put them upside down on a plate to 'sweat'.
2. Chop the flesh coarsely.
3. Melt the butter in a saucepan and add the chopped tomato, parsley and garlic. Cook for 15 minutes over a medium heat and purée this sauce in a sieve or blender. Add the rice and half the cheese and mix together. Season and remove from the heat.
4. Set the oven at 220°C (425°F; gas mark 7). Oil an oven dish.
5. Stuff the tomatoes with the mixture and sprinkle with the remaining Gruyère cheese. Arrange the tomatoes in the dish and place in the oven for 20 minutes, the time necessary to cook the rice.
6. Serve this dish hot, or very cold.

Tomates à la Provençale

Tomatoes with Garlic and Parsley

Serves 4. Preparation: 5 min Cooking: 1 hr 15 min approx

★

- ○ **6 good-sized ripe tomatoes**
- ○ **2 garlic cloves**
- ○ **5ml (1 tsp) chopped parsley**
- ○ **200ml (7 fl oz) olive oil**
- ○ **5ml (1 tsp) sugar**
- ○ **salt and pepper**

1. Wash the tomatoes and cut in half, removing the seeds. Heat the oil in a large frying pan and put in the tomatoes, with the cut surface face downwards. Cover the pan and cook for about 15 minutes over a high heat to ensure that the tomatoes give out all their liquid.
2. Meanwhile, peel and chop the garlic. Mix with the chopped parsley.
3. After 15 minutes of cooking, remove the lid and take the pan from the heat. Turn the tomatoes over carefully and sprinkle each one with 2 pinches of sugar, 3 pinches of garlic and parsley, and 1 pinch of salt and pepper.
4. Put the pan back on a very low heat, cover and cook for 1 hour. When the water from the tomatoes has evaporated, add a few spoonfuls of cold water as necessary. If the tomatoes are large, they may need a further 15 minutes' cooking. Traditionally, the tomatoes should be well-cooked and wrinkled.

These tomatoes can also be cooked in a well-oiled dish containing a little water and placed in a hot oven, but this is not the way it is done in Provence. The garlic and parsley mixture may be replaced by butter and chopped parsley, as they do in Lyons. Or you can season the tomatoes with chopped herbs.

Big round (Marmande) tomatoes can be eaten raw or cooked. The plum variety, which are smaller and longer, are delicious in salads when slightly green, and make wonderful sauces when they are very ripe. To peel them easily, plunge into a saucepan of boiling water for 20 to 30 seconds, then place under cold water: the skin will slide off. Remove the seeds by cutting them in half horizontally, and pressing very gently in the palm of the hand. Do this when preparing tomatoes for salads, stuffings, sauces, casseroles and so on.

Potiron Farci (p73) ▶

Wines: the Finishing Touch

Nowadays excellent quality table wines are within the reach of everyone, though you should expect to pay more for a good vintage wine from one of the famous vineyards, such as Nuits-St-Georges or Schloss Johannisberg Riesling. When buying French wine, look for the *Appellation Contrôlée* label, which is a guarantee of quality.

Below is a guide to the wines that go best with certain foods, but there are no absolute *rules* about which wine to serve with what food – in the end it is your palate that must decide. For a large, formal meal, certain wines traditionally follow each other through the menu and you could serve three or even four wines at one meal. In this case, it is usual to serve dry sherry with the soup, dry white wine with the fish course, claret or burgundy with the meat or game and a white dessert wine or medium sweet champagne with the dessert. For cheese, your guests would return to the claret or burgundy. Certain foods kill the flavour of wine and should therefore be avoided if you are planning to serve wine with the meal. Mint sauce, for example, or any salad with a strong vinaigrette dressing, will destroy the taste of the wine.

Remember that red wines are generally served *chambré*, or at room temperature, to bring out the flavour. Draw the cork at least three or four hours before you plan to drink the wine and let the bottle stand in the kitchen or a warm room. (Never be tempted into putting the bottle in hot water or in front of the fire – the flavour will be ruined.) The exception to the *chambré* rule is Beaujolais, which can be served cool – some people even serve it chilled. White or rosé wines are usually served chilled – the easiest way is to put them in the fridge an hour before serving, or plunge them into an ice bucket, if you have one. Champagne should also be served well chilled and is generally brought to the table in an ice bucket.

Wines to Serve with Food

Oysters, shellfish	Chablis, dry Moselle, Champagne
Fried or grilled fish	Dry Graves, Moselle, Hock, Rosé, Blanc de Blanc
Fish with sauces	Riesling, Pouilly-Fuissé, Chablis
Veal, pork or chicken dishes (served simply)	Rosé, Riesling, a light red wine such as Beaujolais
Chicken or pork served with a rich sauce	Claret, Côte de Rhône, Médoc
Rich meat dishes, steaks, game	Red Burgundy, Rioja, Red Chianti
Lamb or duck	Claret, Beaujolais
Desserts and puddings	White Bordeaux, Sauternes, Entre Deux Mers
Cheese	Burgundy, Rioja, Cabernet Sauvignon

Published for Selectabook Ltd 1992 by Wordsworth Editions Ltd,
8b East Street, Ware, Hertfordshire.

Copyright © Wordsworth Editions Ltd 1992.

Designed by Tony Selina, The Old Goat Graphic Company,
London, England.

ISBN 1-85326-982-4

Printed and bound in Hong Kong by South China Printing Company.